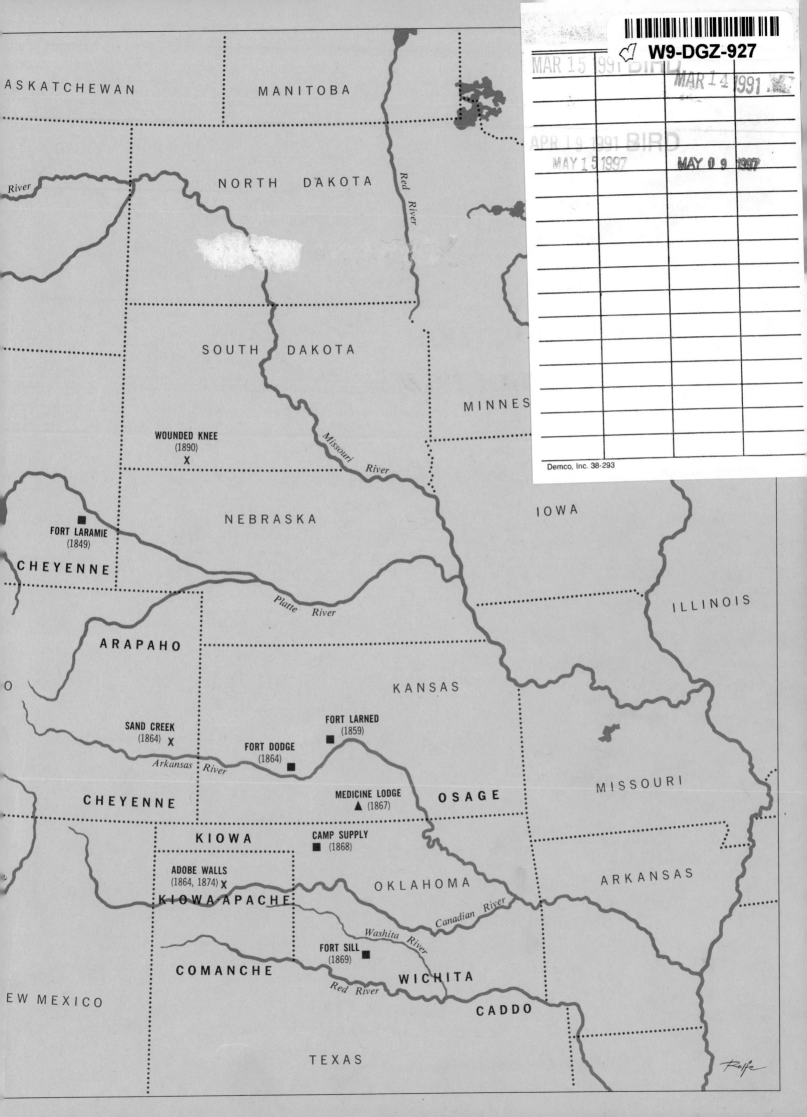

SASKATCHEWAN

MANITOBA

NORTH DAKOTA

Red River

SOUTH DAKOTA

Missouri River

MINNES

WOUNDED KNEE
(1890)
X

NEBRASKA

IOWA

FORT LARAMIE
(1849)

CHEYENNE

Platte River

ARAPAHO

ILLINOIS

KANSAS

SAND CREEK
(1864) X

FORT LARNED
(1859)

FORT DODGE
(1864)

Arkansas River

MISSOURI

CHEYENNE

MEDICINE LODGE
▲ (1867)

OSAGE

KIOWA

CAMP SUPPLY
■ (1868)

ADOBE WALLS
(1864, 1874) X

KIOWA-APACHE

OKLAHOMA

ARKANSAS

Canadian River

Washita River

FORT SILL
(1869)

COMANCHE

WICHITA

Red River

NEW MEXICO

CADDO

TEXAS

Rolfe

WILL SOULE: INDIAN PHOTOGRAPHER AT FORT SILL

WILL SOULE

Indian Photographer at
Fort Sill, Oklahoma 1869-74

by

RUSSELL E. BELOUS and ROBERT A. WEINSTEIN

The Ward Ritchie Press · 1969

To the numberless photographers
of the American West, past and present,
whose brilliant graphic images
document and illuminate the struggles
of Americans for a future grounded
in freedom and equal opportunity

ACKNOWLEDGEMENT

The authors wish to acknowledge gratefully their large debt, principally to Mr. Gillett Griswold, Director of the Fort Sill Museum at Fort Sill, Oklahoma, whose careful, exhaustive study of the life and work of William S. Soule was generously and open-handedly shared with us without reserve. No work on Soule or his photographs could afford to be undertaken without recognition of Mr. Griswold's effective pioneer work in this field.

Many kind individuals and generous institutions have been of serious assistance to the authors in preparing this work for publication. Outstanding has been Mr. Armando Solis, Chief Photographer, Los Angeles County Museum of Natural History whose demonstrated excellence in printing the 100-year-old wet-plate collodion negatives is unsurpassed. Dr. Edwin Carpenter, Western Bibliographer of the Huntington Library, San Marino, California, happily drew the author's attention to the Soule photographs among the General Philip Reade Collection in their possession. Mr. Michael Harrison of Sacramento, California, Mrs. Alys Frese, Director of the Western History Room at the Denver Public Library, Denver, Colorado, and the many warm colleagues whose willingness to read our manuscripts and contribute suggestions of worth are deeply appreciated by the authors.

It is especially necessary to thank the entire staff of the History Division, Los Angeles County Museum of Natural History, who, under the direction of the Chief Curator, Ruth I. Mahood, assisted in many helpful ways, including the ever-tedious task of typing interminable drafts of manuscripts.

Special consideration must be rendered the many unknown American Indian informants whose knowledge, freely given, made possible many individual identifications among Soule's portraits as well as additional information otherwise completely unavailable.

For the inevitable errors that will certainly, and regrettably, be discovered in this work the authors wish to accept full responsibility. It would be greatly appreciated if corrections of errors and additional useful information would be made available to the authors.

PREFACE

Ralph Linton, in reviewing the dynamics of culture, once observed that "culture is infinitely perfectible." And so it must have seemed both to the Native Americans and to the invaders of their land. For nearly every conflicting group it was a world of closed societies and locally specialized cultures providing each individual a single, more or less consistent configuration of absolute ethical, religious and aesthetic standards. Then, as now, missionaries struck out to new lands, and expansionist governments imposed alien codes of law. Traveling artists and photographers, revealing fresh interpretations of beauty (and ugliness), showed alternative custom in action. In response nearly always did each ethnic group defend itself initially with ethnocentric armor—the deeply entrenched premises, values and goals which had the stamp of high ethics and religion.

While the American Indian was neither the first, nor will he be the last, to experience the cultural shock of change, his experiences have been the subject of intense study by the social scientist. The New World, as a microcosm of world contact, continues to provide important clues as to possible future longer-term trends. Perhaps the central question was (and is): can there yet be an accommodation of the many diverse cultures? Can an increasingly complex society encourage (or permit) the development of flexible personalities and allow more scope for private or optional behavior?

As the American Indian became a minority in his own land, his cultures underwent many tests of their survival value in the face of new technological pressures and under the impact of many new and alternative possibilities in behavior. In this respect his problems were similar to those of other minority groups, particularly the Mexican-American and Negro. All were, in addition, caught up in the essential conflict of Anglo-American paradox dogma: accommodate yourselves quickly (join the melting-pot), yet maintain a competitive, individualistic spirit. Until the Indian Reorganization Act of 1934, it was the official policy of the United States Government to "encourage" accommodation by destroying the tribal organization; while at the same time individualism was effectively countered by the United States Army during the last half of the 19th century.

Today, in 1968, there still remains for all of us a challenge. For in spite of past indignities there are still rich tapestries of regional and local traditions, in this country and abroad, nourished by people who believe that their cultures can be successfully integrated into the mass-produced society. If the history of this country seems to belie this confidence, then perhaps one of us is wrong. We would hope that it is our historical interpretation that needs re-study. For if Linton was right then it is clear that we cannot now imagine the numerous lines of behavioral experiment which man, if he survives self-destruction, will have explored a hundred, a thousand, a million years from now. Perhaps however from some vantage point in the future, a culture historian will label peoples living in this era as the last examples of *Homo* as a predominantly regional and local animal.

We hope not.

TABLE OF CONTENTS

LIST OF PLATES

THE AMERICAN INDIAN: THE IMAGE APPEARS

BY RUSSELL E. BELOUS

It may not be an exaggeration to suppose that if there had never been an American Indian, then he would have had to have been invented. Indeed it sometimes seems as though he had, for the difference between myth and reality is often a meager one. President John F. Kennedy once wrote: "For a subject worked and reworked so often in novels, motion pictures, and television, American Indians remain probably the least understood and most misunderstood Americans of us all." If the following pages show that this native American *was* a reality and can be understood, then we will have accomplished our purpose. It may seem difficult to imagine that the publication of this unique collection of glass plates, nearly 100 years old, reflecting a most candid photographic study of individuals, could provide the impetus to this knowledge. These are the same Indians who, after pausing momentarily before William Soule's camera, would take up again their varied battle cries; and herein is the importance of this negative collection in contributing to a reality which for nearly four centuries the white man had missed finding.

If these many years of study have not brought adequate understanding (or reality) to this subject, it is not because of lack of interest. At vari-ous times in the young history of this country, representatives of nearly every group of newly-arrived Americans wrestled with the question: soldier, farmer, businessman, adventurer, explorer, statesman, churchman, and academician. Each saw the Indian in a different image, according to his own immediate needs or desires. Before we compare these many diverse images with those of Will Soule's, let us look back a bit into time. Who were the ancestors of these Indians, the people who sat in front of his camera one hundred years ago?

Some 35,000 years ago, they had come out of Asia to the New World—the continent of North America. Although cut off from the Near and Far East centers of development by the two great oceans, they achieved much in their isolation. The nature of their independent discoveries and inventions, many of which were to rival those of the Old World, have long been the cause of intense speculation. They result in many fancy theories about the origin of the American Indian. Even their name springs from a mis-apprehension on the part of Christopher Columbus. At various times, there have been attempts to establish that they were descendants of the Ten Lost Tribes of Israel, stragglers from the fleet of Alexander the Great, or emigrants from the mythical continent of Atlantis or a similarly hypothetical Pacific island called Mu. These first settlers of America undoubtedly came by way of Alaska to this continent already equipped with tools, fire, and language.

It seems likely that the first wave of migrants followed the coastal plain, north and east to the valley of the Mackenzie. There was an ice-free corridor along the eastern side of the Rockies and also plenty of game. As nomadic hunters and fishermen, they began to make their way south to the Plains regions, where they found a land abounding in game and free from human enemies. The population of the continent was very early divided into two recognizable culture complexes: the seed-gatherers of the Rocky Mountain Plateau west to California and east across Texas; the game hunters centered in the High Plains of the Western United States with some penetration into the Eastern Woodlands and toward the Texas border.

The invention of agriculture in the Old World had ushered in a great period in human history. It transformed *homo sapiens* from one of the rarest to the most numerous of mammalian species and resulted in a tremendous acceleration in the rate of cultural development. This was no less true in the New World. By 1000 B.C., maize had found a favorable environment in Middle America and at the time of the arrival of the white man, the first reshuffling of the population under the impact of agriculture had already taken place. Settled life in semi-permanent villages, supported by agriculture, had spread as far north as the crops would support it. A series of regional culture patterns had emerged, linked with particular climatic and environmental areas. The predominantly hunting or fishing cultures included the Eskimo, Northeast Woodlands, Plains, and Northwest Coast. In the remaining areas, Southeast Woodlands, Rocky Mountain Plateau, Southwest and California, vegetable food was most important, with incidental dependence on hunting and/or fishing.

So for thousands of years the American Indian was alone, save for a few visitors from Polynesia and Northern Europe. In the year 1492, these diverse North American tribes numbered about a million people. In temperament they ranged from the peaceful Pima of Arizona to the belligerent Iroquois of New York. Some were town dwellers, others nomadic hunters. The Shoshoni of the Plateau, living in comparative isolation, hunting deer and gathering wild seeds and piñon nuts were in contrast to the enormously skilled maritime people of the Northwest Coast. Separated from the rainy forests of the Northwest by the Rockies, the Plains stretched east and southeast, an almost limitless expanse of grasslands rolling all the way from the mountains to the Mississippi. Until the horse was introduced by the Spanish, the Plains were quiet. Farming tribes—the Mandan and the Arikara—led a settled existence along the rivers of the region and occasionally hunted buffalo. The huge herds that wandered through this area were

also followed by nomads, the Comanche and Apache, but hunting the buffalo on foot yielded too small a reward either to attract or to sustain a large population.

East of the plains, the forests of the Eastern Woodlands reached from the Mississippi to the Atlantic Coast. Here were the tribes so well known in America's colonial history: Mohegan, Delaware, Iroquois, Mohawk, Oneida. Banding together, they built a successful political system, a confederation, which endured for at least two centuries.

Scarcely less formidable than the Iroquois were the warlike Muskhogean tribes of the Southeastern region, the Creek confederacy, the Chickasaw and Choctaw. In the mountains of what was to become Georgia and the Carolinas, were the Cherokee, an agricultural tribe. One influential tribe of the Muskhogean family, the Natchez, inherited a mound-building tradition that began over 2,000 years ago in the Ohio Valley. These "temple mound" people offered a complex, class-structured society and the only absolute monarchy known among the North American Indians.

But the Indian's cultural diversity and his lack of inter-regional political organizations were contributing factors in his eventual destruction. In addition, however, there was in the Indian's homelands a geography advantageous to the enterprising adventurers from the Old World. Once the white man had mastered the Atlantic, the continent lay open to his grasp. The explorers who reconnoitered the highly indented and hospitable eastern coast of North America found bays, harbors, inlets and rivers that offered attractive sites for initial settlement and, later on, easy access to the interior. As the relatively narrow Tidewater Belt of the Atlantic became crowded and its thin soil depleted, the Piedmont, extending to the Appalachian Mountains, was soon occupied.

While the Piedmont was a temporary barrier to the English colonists, there were two gateways: the valleys of the Hudson and Mohawk to the west, and the Hudson-Champlain passage to the north. The western route was the great Iroquois war trail. Southward from Pennsylvania stretched the Shenandoah Valley. It offered an indirect way west to the Cumberland Gap and then out to the more open country beyond. The French and Spaniards were even better favored by nature for their advances into the great central basin drained by the Mississippi. In the north, the St. Lawrence provided a route around one end of the Appalachian barrier; in the south, the Alabama Black Belt and the entire Gulf Coast offered easy passage around the other end. In brief, these were the people and the country to which the European came.

In retrospect, it may appear that the long occupancy of the Indian tribes had left little imprint on the present culture of North America. With the exception of many local crops, most of which have now been incorporated into world agriculture, and the sharing of knowledge of techniques for dealing with a new territory which the aborigines offered the early settlers, the Indian population appears to have made little contribution in the north. However, it may be significant that the pattern of confederacy which was widespread on the North American continent has rarely emerged elsewhere. Confederacies, as opposed to empires, are characterized by the importance attached to individual initiative and freedom of choice. It is at least interesting to speculate that the establishment of the confederacy which became the United States of America may have had its roots in aboriginal patterns, and that the tradition of democracy and individual freedom flourished with special vigor in the land which the proud and independent Indian had prepared for us.

While today's ethnologist still probes and searches for the *real* Amerindian, it is always of interest to the ethno-historian that we chronicle the European's many images of America's native population. That these images were altered by time is a reflection of the changing ideological moods of the Old World immigrants and their subsequent experiences on this new continent.

Christopher Columbus' first reports of the New World and its people were contained in two letters written in February and early March, 1493, in the course of the return trip from his voyage of discovery. On his way to Spain, he touched at Lisbon and the two letters were transferred to a courier to be rushed overland to the Spanish court. By June of that year, a number of editions were available to the public: "As soon as I had landed on the first island that I encountered in that sea I had several Indians taken prisoner.... [they were] ...a well-formed people and of fair stature ... very comely." From this time on the image of the New World would cause profound changes in the Old. Portugal was soon locked in a diplomatic struggle with Spain over rights to the new discovery. Portugal, the great seafaring nation, had obtained various guarantees in the realms of the farther oceans that were supported by papal bulls and the formal Treaty of Alcacovas. By the summer of 1493, new papal bulls were undermining Portugal's position, and Columbus was on his way back to the Indies with a hastily assembled expedition to seal the Spanish claim with commerce and colonies. The Treaty of Tordesillas, in 1494, giving Portugal the hump of Brazil, was only the first of many American matters to occupy the chief statesmen of Europe.

Rich America played a part of many sides in the Reformation; in the expansion of the fur trade so important in the lives of England, France, and Russia; in the rise of English and Dutch mercantilism; and even in the foundation of modern international law. In many respects the peculiar character of the American Indians was of importance in world affairs. They often welcomed their conquerors and helped the young European colonies. Their impact was considerable in the spread to Europe of such Indian crops and products as corn, tomatoes, rubber, white potatoes, tobacco, medicinal drugs, peanuts, chewing gum and chocolate. Their character became profoundly operative on the European mind: it was their "childlikeness" that most of the first Spanish reports described. The famous *Essays* of Michel Eyquem de Montaigne published in France in the 1580's read in part: "I find ...

there is nothing in that nation [the New World], that is either barbarous or savage, unlesse men call that barbarisme which is not common to them. . . . It is a nation, would I answer Plato, that hath no kinde of traffike, no knowledge of Letters, no intelligence of numbers, . . . no use of service, or riches or of povertie; no contracts, no successions, no partitions, no occupation but idle; no respect of kindred, but common, no use of wine, corne, or mettle."

These same thoughts, by 1750, were expressed by Jean Jacques Rousseau as he envisioned the blessed state of the man, the noble savage, pure, simple, and above all free. The pioneer American anthropologist, Lewis Henry Morgan, was impressed by the propertyless society of the American Indian; ". . . A mere property career is not the final destiny of mankind, if progress is to be the law of the future as it has been in the past. . . ." So too for Karl Marx and Friedrich Engels. The latter, in his *The Origin of the Family, Private Property and the State*, published in 1884, described the notion he had of the Indian way of life: "And a wonderful constitution it is. . . . No soldiers, no gendarmes or police, ... There cannot be any poor or needy . . . . And what men and women such a society breeds is proved by the admiration inspired in all white people who have come into contact with unspoiled Indians, by the personal dignity, uprightness, strength of character and courage of these barbarians. . . ."

If the image of the American Indian had an effect on the changing world of Europe and also in the peoples who came to the Americas, what was it that made them so different? While the answer is complex we may note that an important difference was in their view of property: cooperation in the use of property in common as against the general European view of competition for the acquisition of private property. The Indian world seemed to be devoted to living, the European world to getting. Thomas Jefferson suggested to several Indian chiefs that ". . . temperance, peace and agriculture . . . will prepare you to possess property . . ." Bishop Landa, among others, was disturbed and frustrated by the Indians' "indolence." Why couldn't they work? Why didn't they want to labor to acquire things?

The gulf between the Indian and the white view of life was at its most unbridgeable in the region that became the United States, colonized by a people to whom diligence, labor, and thrift became the highest virtues, and work was literally man's sacred calling. In Protestant North America, the Indian nations were deliberately stamped out to the point that they became the Vanishing American. It was generally believed that some natural laws were at work by which the Indians automatically perished under the withering touch of civilization. Their image changed: the noble savage gave way to the bloodthirsty savage; the barbarian gave way to the Red Brother asking for Guidance of the missionaries. But then, they were still romantic heroes to many; and the mid-19th century found its Indian heroes in fact, as well as in Fenimore Cooper fiction. In certain areas the Indian attracted the mystics, and they often played a part in the founding of various religious sects. In the various conflicting images, the Indian was sometimes wise, often dour and humorless, his savagery sometimes a romantic virtue.

As the Vanishing American Indian vanished from the eastern states, he became a figure of nostalgic folklore. Admirable as some of these images might have been, by the mid-19th century the Indian problem was an economic matter to be handled as economically as possible. The Indians were now mostly west of the Mississippi and, as exiles, they came to start life over again. But for them the story began anew; and ironically, although declining in force and influence in America's history, they still managed to produce for nearly four decades some of the most stirring images of all.

Historians have long examined and speculated on the causes of the tragic Indian Wars of the late 19th century. Since it was *this* war that William Soule had stumbled upon and had subsequently produced *his* images of a part of it, it will be of interest here to look at two aspects of that conflict. First, in what ways did the attitude and policies of the United States Government affect the Indian, and, secondly, how did the Indian react to these policies?

Upon achieving independence, the United States became the possessor of several native policies inherited from the colonial period. On the one hand stood Britain's "imperial" policy which had sought to conciliate native groups in order to provide stability and encourage commerce and on the other was the "European settler's" policy which had sought the removal of the natives and the acquisition of the land by the newly arrived settlers. During the initial period of weakness, the United States admitted, in effect, that it had not acquired complete ownership of, or even control over, the regions quitclaimed by the British in 1783, and that it was necessary to negotiate with the tribes. Nevertheless, this de facto recognition of tribal quasi-independence was not based upon any desire to uphold the principle of self-determination for small nations. As rapidly as the balance of power in any given region tipped in favor of the federal government, the United States crushed the respective native groups and broke treaties as it saw fit.

The Indian policy of the United States during this period was somewhat ambiguous and contradictory. On the one hand it sought to conciliate the more powerful of the native states while, on the other, her citizens were pressing for the acquisition of more land. No better illustration of the disparity that existed between pronouncements and deeds can be found than in the writings and policy of Thomas Jefferson. In his second Inaugural Address, March 1805, he said: "The aboriginal inhabitants . . . I have regarded with the commiseration their history inspires. Endowed with the faculties and the rights of men, breathing an ardent love of liberty and independence . . . the stream of overflowing population from other regions directed itself on these shores . . . [and] they have been overwhelmed; . . . now reduced within limits too narrow for the hunter's state, humanity enjoins us to teach them agriculture and the domestic arts. . . . We have therefore liberally furnished them with implements and instructors . . . and they are covered with the aegis of the law against aggressors from among ourselves. But the endeavors to enlighten them . . . have powerful obstacles to encounter; they are combated . . . [by the Indians' ignorance, pride, and habits and by leaders who] inculcate a sanctimonious reverence for the customs of their ancestors . . . . they too have their antiphilosophists . . . who dread reformation. . . ."

The expected French acquisition of Louisiana led Jefferson to begin acquiring, as rapidly as possible, all Indian lands east of the Mississippi. By 1809, more than 100 million acres were acquired by intimidation, bribery, questionable treaties, and dubious procedures. In 1817, President James Monroe said: "The hunter state can exist only in the vast uncultivated desert. It yields to the . . . greater force of civilized population; and, of right, it ought to yield, for the earth was given to mankind to support the greater number of which it is capable; and no tribe or people have a right to withhold from the wants of others, more than is necessary for their support and comfort." (This statement is especially interesting today when the citizens of the United States have great wealth while others live in poverty and overpopulated areas.) In 1830, President Andrew Jackson persuaded Congress to pass legislation authorizing the President "to exchange the public domain in the West for Indian lands in the East, (and) to give perpetual title to the country thus exchanged. . . ." But, twenty-four years later, the Kansas-Nebraska Act doomed the Indian Territory concept, with all of its pledges of "perpetual title."

A change had come over America during this first half of the 19th century, even while the picturesque Plains life was reaching its apogee. By now the Indian's image had been well fixed by the adventurous artist, for it was still too early for the camera. Among those who sought for his likeness were: John Trumbull (1790), Charles Bird King (1821), George Catlin (1830), Alfred Jacob Miller (1837), Samuel Seymour (1819), Charles Bodmer (1833), John Mix Stanley (1843), J. O. Lewis (1835). But time was running out for both the artist *and* the Indian. The United States, once a small country east of the Mississippi, glad of a buffer state to defend it from Spain, now saw itself as stretching from coast to coast. There were gold-miners in Colorado and California and homesteaders in Oregon. Even though some of them did not then want to colonize the Indian country, they called for a safe stagecoach service across it and, ultimately, for railroads. Moreover, the country itself was being whittled down. By 1830, the lands east of the Mississippi were being carved up into states, and the Indians there began to move west into the near empty hunting country.

By 1849, the War Department turned the whole Indian problem over to the Department of Interior. It was understood that the duty of this department was to get all Indians settled on reservations and out of the white man's way. The Indians of the Plains were largely unaware of the massive changes about to take place. In 1851, the Commissioner of Indian Affairs, Luke Lea wrote: ". . . on the general subject of the civilization of the Indians, many and diversified opinions have been put forth; but, unfortunately, like the race to which they relate, they are too wild to be of much utility. . . . [a proper program should provide for] their concentration, their domestication and their ultimate incorporation into the great body of our citizen population."

For the next fifteen years or so Indian attacks, peace treaties, and attacks on the Indians followed each other in fantastic succession. It was the attitude of the military that the Indians should be "whipped to a standstill," then fed until they either "began to earn an honest living" or died out. The Department of Interior believed that the red man could be coaxed and educated into white ways. The alternatives were few, equally difficult and morally disastrous. Could millions of acres in the Plains have been left undeveloped, in the middle of a growing country, for the pleasure of a few thousand hunters? That would have been impossible. The tide of immigration from the Old World and across the New was such that no man could stop it. The alternative to the liquidation of the Indian would have been large-scale rural redevelopment. But this was unknown to 19th-century lawmakers and so they made hopeful treaties which they seldom had the ability or the moral courage to carry out. The new treaties did not merely ask the Indians to remain within boundaries while the white men passed; they marked off reservations which were not large enough for hunting but only for farming and cattle-raising on land of dubious value for either. The horse and buffalo days seemed over, and some Indians accepted the reservation. The old men put away the medicine bundles and soon refused to teach the young people any Indian lore. "Better to turn around," they said, "and lead a new life." Many could see nothing good in the new life. Said Red Cloud, the Sioux: "Friends, it has been our misfortune to welcome the white man. We have been deceived. He brought with him some shining things that pleased our eyes; he brought weapons more effective than our own. Above all he brought the spirit-water that makes one forget old age, weakness and sorrow. But I wish to say to you that if you wish to possess these things for yourselves, you must begin anew and put away the wisdom of your fathers. You must lay up food and forget the hungry. When your house is built, your storeroom filled, then look around for a neighbor whom you can take advantage of and seize all he has."

The general pattern of the Indian's displacement had been set by the government at a conference with the northern tribes at Fort Laramie, Wyoming, in 1851. The Indians were to receive $50,000 a year for fifteen years in return for which they were to allow roads and military posts within their country. The Indians soon found that each fort in their country meant more forts, more soldiers, more travelers. The buffalo began to disappear at a surprising rate, and soon every move the Indian made seemed to be interfered with, thus causing the response from them in the one way they knew well. The war parties now were not a mere handful of men out for glory. Nor was war any longer a game. Today we call such desperate men "guerrilla fighters," making war their one business in life and clinging to a leader as their only salvation.

Commissioner Lea had earlier expressed a viewpoint that was to become dominant after 1870. The native groups were to be concentrated on small reserves, they were to be "domesticated"—in effect a policy of enforced acculturation; or, as the Secretary of the Interior Caleb B. Smith said in 1862: "Instead of being treated as independent nations [as in the past] they should be regarded as wards of the Government. . . ."

A new era in federal policy toward the Indian began in 1870-71. Former Indian Commissioner John Collier refers to one facet of this policy: "Beginning about 1870, a leading aim of the United States was to destroy the Plains Indians' societies through destroying their religions; and it may be that the world has never witnessed a religious persecution so implacable and so variously implemented." Native groups were placed in concentration camps, shifted about at the whim of bureaucrats, starved, intimidated, and persecuted. Their religious ceremonies were forcibly suppressed, and every effort was made to destroy their secular cultural heritage as well. In addition, the administrators of the program were often corrupt, and supplies intended for the impoverished natives ended up in the hands of whites.

In 1871, the United States Congress decided that "no Indian Nation or Tribe within the territory of the United States shall be acknowledged or recognized as an independent nation, tribe or power with whom the United States may contract by treaty. . . ." This decision was not without its problems since there were still several independent tribes and a number of previously subdued groups who possessed no treaty protections. These tribes without treaties especially were to suffer after 1871, being deprived of their land without compensation and being offered only minimal and belated federal assistance. In 1872, General Francis C. Walker, Commissioner of Indian Affairs, expressed the government's native policy as follows: "There is no question of national dignity, be it remembered, involved in the treatment of savages by civilized powers. With wild men, as with wild beasts, the question of whether in a given situation one shall fight,

coax, or run, is a question merely of what is easiest and safest. . . . [T]he Indians should be made as comfortable on and as uncomfortable off, their reservation as possible. . . ." General Walker, in carrying out his government's paternalistic policy, concluded: "Every year's advance of our frontier takes in a territory as large as some of the kingdoms in Europe. We are richer by hundreds of millions, the Indian is poorer by a large part of the little that he has. This growth is bringing imperial greatness to the nation; to the Indian it brings wretchedness, destitution, beggary."

By 1881, President Arthur would admit: "We have to deal with the appalling fact that though thousands of lives have been sacrificed and hundreds of millions of dollars expended in the attempt to solve the Indian problem, it has until within the past few years seemed scarcely nearer a solution than it was half a century ago." Paternalism culminated in the passage of the Dawes Act of 1887, which established the policy of breaking up reservations into individual homesteads. This was an attempt to "civilize" the Indian by merging him into the body politic of the nation. It was based on the "Protestant ethic" premise that ownership of real estate was a moral good, fostering thrift, industry, and providing the spark of energy or ambition that leads to wealth and prestige. Churchmen and reformers had urged what they believed to be a humane policy toward the nation's wards. Statesmen like Carl Schurz, religious leaders like Bishop Henry B. Whipple, literary figures like Helen Hunt Jackson, whose *Century of Dishonor* (1881) stirred the nation's conscience, were loud in their criticism of the government's treatment of the Indian, and their attitudes were effective in bringing about important changes in policy. It was impossible to imagine that these well-intentioned liberal, and sometimes radical critics, would contribute to a system in which the Indian often faced the alternative of either living in a tribal slum on the prairie or becoming an unwilling homesteader. But then we have managed to make the same error, in modern times, with another of America's minorities—the Negro. They are denied their ambition to participate on equal terms in American civilization; the Indian, who desired above all to continue his own way of life, was deprived of hunting grounds which would have made that possible, and was pressured to "settle down" and become "good" farmers and citizens.

Before that pressure could be exerted, the Indian had to be defeated in battle; and herein lies the central plot for countless stories about the Indian Wars: fact or fiction, real or imagined, good or bad, simple or complex.

Indians of the Great Plains and the Rocky Mountains, about 225,000 in number, presented a formidable obstacle to white settlement. The strongest and most warlike were the Sioux, Blackfoot, Crow, Cheyenne, Arapaho, and Nez Percé in the north; the Comanche, Apache, Ute, Kiowa, Southern Cheyenne and Southern Arapaho in the south and center. Mounted on swift horses, well armed for plains warfare, and living on the herds of buffalo that roamed the open range, these tribes long maintained a stubborn resistance to white penetration of their hunting grounds. The first serious invasion of these hunting grounds came with the great migration of the 1840's. The advance of miners into the mountains, the building of transcontinental railroads in the late 1860's and the invasion of the grasslands by cattlemen threatened every western tribe with the same fate as that which had nearly decimated the California Indian.

Until 1861 the Great Plains had been relatively peaceful, but in that year the invasion of Colorado by thousands of miners and the advance of white settlers along the upper Mississippi and Missouri began a series of armed clashes. The Dakota Sioux in 1862 devastated the Minnesota frontier and massacred or captured almost 1,000 settlers. On the southern plains, the Cheyenne, Arapaho, Comanche and Kiowa fought Union and Confederate troops alike during the Civil War. When Colorado volunteer troops nearly exterminated Black Kettle's Sand Creek camp in 1864, news of the tragedy spread to the Northern Cheyenne and the Sioux; their retaliation was

quick. In spite of the 1865 treaty with the Sioux which obtained passage of the Bozeman Trail into the gold fields of western Montana, and, in 1867, the Medicine Lodge Treaty, warfare continued. In December 1866 Captain William J. Fetterman, stationed at Fort Phil Kearny, Wyoming, was ambushed by Red Cloud, and his command of eighty men were killed. Fort Buford, on the Missouri just across the Montana line, was sniped at by the Sioux in 1867. The American public, more concerned till now about the problems of reconstruction, was stirred up by a report of a "horrible massacre" at Fort Buford which actually never took place. It was a report which the commissioner of Indian affairs attributed to the "rapacity and rascality of frontier settlers, whose interests are to bring on a war and supply our armies . . . at exorbitant prices." In any case pitched battles did occur, nearly 200 of them in the years 1869-1876.

Historians have long speculated on whether the final results would have been different if the various Indian tribes had been able effectively to unite. Perhaps they might have tired out the United States, (as white resistance to reconstruction was doing in the South); but no Tecumseh, no Prophet appeared. With rare exceptions the Indian was divided into small parcels and defeated piecemeal.

The death knell of the Sioux was struck in 1875 when prospectors discovered gold in the Black Hills of South Dakota. These hills, to the Sioux, were holy ground which the government had promised to retain for them inviolate. For one summer General Sheridan was able to hold back the greedy gold seekers, but in the following spring they broke through. Under Sitting Bull and Crazy Horse the Sioux struck back. The resulting campaign of the 7th Cavalry in the following year is well known to almost everyone. It was on the Little Big Horn that the Custer legend began—when he, and his entire command of nearly 300 officers and men were surrounded and killed by the braves led by Crazy Horse. When, several months later, Colonel Nelson A. Miles caught up with and defeated him, hostilities on the northern plains were nearly at an end.

The final act was the surrender of Sitting Bull in 1881.

Now more and more Indians were driven from their ancient homes. In Montana and Colorado the vast holdings of the Crow, Blackfoot, and Ute were confiscated and opened to settlement. The discovery of gold on the Salmon river in western Idaho precipitated an invasion of the peaceful Nez Percé homelands. They refused to surrender lands guaranteed to them, and the federal government in 1877 decided to drive them out. Chief Joseph struck back, but in vain, and then conducted 200 braves and 600 squaws and papooses on a fighting retreat over 1,500 miles of mountain and plain, a memorable feat in the annals of Indian warfare. On October 5, 1877, just short of asylum in Canada, Chief Joseph surrendered. He said: "Hear me, my chiefs. I am tired; my heart is sick and sad. From where the sun now stands I will fight no more, forever."

Although it would be nearly ten years before the Apache chief, Geronimo, surrendered, Chief Joseph spoke for the entire Indian nation. By the middle eighties virtually all the hostile tribes were confined to specific reservations. The buffalo was gone, and the Indians became totally dependent on the government and its Indian agents for nearly all their subsistence. Many were driven to desperation by dishonest or incompetent agents, arbitrary regulation, the steady shrinkage of their lands, and, most of all, by the attack on the basic social, economic, and political institutions of the tribe.

Bleak prospects for the future combined with nostalgic memories of the past to produce a state of mind particularly susceptible to a Messianic fervor that swept the western reservations in 1889 and 1890. A strange mixture of Christianity and paganism, the Ghost Dance religion promised a return of the old order and the disappearance of the white race. This religious militancy provoked a call for military protection. On December 29, at Wounded Knee, South Dakota, soldiers of Colonel James W. Forsyth's 7th Cavalry tried to disarm Big Foot's band of Sioux, who had fled from the Cheyenne River Reservation. The resulting battle, or massacre if you prefer, caused the death of many Indian women and children. It has always served as a tragic reminder that it was this that marked the close of the Indian wars.

THE AMERICAN INDIAN: THE IMAGE FIXED

BY ROBERT A. WEINSTEIN

The practice of photography was only 22 years old in 1861, the opening year of the Civil

Medicine Bluff near Fort Sill, Indian Territory

The Indian wars on the Southern Plains in the United States provided the time, the locale, the events and the people for Will Soule's photographic "drama" of the Southern Plains Indians: the Kiowa, Kiowa-Apache, the Cheyenne, the Comanche, the Apache, the Wichita, the Caddo and the Arapaho.

The time began for Will Soule late in the fall of 1868, at Fort Dodge, Kansas, followed quickly in turn by a winter stay with General Philip Sheridan's campaigning troops at Camp Supply in Indian Territory. From there, Will Soule accompanied the troops to the newly-building Fort Sill in Oklahoma, deep in Kiowa and Comanche territory, where he remained through the mid-year of 1874.

He photographed the construction of the fort for the United States Army as well as some of the many personalities and events concerned with Fort Sill in those founding years. He left Oklahoma Territory late in 1874 or early in 1875 to return to his home in Boston.

Soule's remaining work is a vivid series of images of one terrifyingly real aspect of the prolonged, tragic Indian Wars on the Southern Plains.

War. Although newly discovered, its technical development was rapid and its popular acceptance was widespread. It had quickly passed through its succeeding stages of growth, marked in turn by daguerreotypes, ambrotypes, ferrotypes, paper negatives and paper prints. In 1861 the making of glass, wet-plate collodion negatives and paper contact prints was well advanced. This wet-plate process used by photographers serving both armies of the Civil War was to a large degree successful in replacing the time-honored "artist-correspondent." It succeeded as well in presenting to the public for the first time in history the true horror of modern warfare. Corpse-littered battlefields, filthy living conditions, sickening medical facilities, exhausted, wounded, and dying soldiers could now be seen by the noncombatants in all of their cold, pitiless reality.

The camera had been successfully used for the first time as a "news gatherer" during the Civil War. Now its potential for more rapid communication of information about people, places and events was assured. The period of intensive, photographic documentation of the American scene was on stage, charged and anxious to get going.

The various photographic corps of all the armies developed many first-rate photographers during the war. Best known were the more celebrated photographers working for and with Matthew Brady. At war's end, some of these men—Alexander Gardner, A. J. Russel, Timothy H. O'Sullivan, and others—turned to the American West for new opportunities for photographic achievements.

The wounded nation's new preoccupation with a transcontinental railroad helped many of them find their way west. The United States Government was busily forming survey parties. Released from battle commitments the army could once again take up the unfinished job of exploring and mapping the Great West. Photographic evidence of this Great West was fast becoming convincing testimony for skeptical Senatorial and House committees.

Newly-formed railroad companies often included "official" photographers to record their building efforts and progress, as well as revealing the real estate opportunities in the growing rights-of-way alongside the westbound rails. The construction of the Union Pacific Railroad west from Omaha, joining with the Central Pacific, building east from Sacramento, was opening the Great Plains and the Pacific slope for expansion and American and foreign capital investment.

Information about the new West was urgently needed. Numerous surveys, official and private, were busy exploring and recording. Reports of every kind abounded. The flood of information and myth about the Great American West was in full flower in 1869.

Most reports were long, wordy, and, in the main, laborious reading. The new element in reporting was the visual record made possible by the camera. As adequate methods for printing photographs had not yet been developed, drawings, engravings, and lithographs made from photographs frequently accompanied reports. Official United States Government reports often included portfolios of mounted photographic prints, 11″ x 14″ or larger. Such photographs— "the real thing"—were very impressive to all who saw them. The names and the reputations of the new Western photographers were fast becoming

important. The call to photograph the new frontier was becoming loud and clarion.

The West, as it does today, meant different things to different people. There was the West of the Rocky Mountains, the great canyons, the gorges, the broad plains, the mighty rivers and the natural thermal wonders of the Yellowstone. There was the California West of the gold mines, the fertile fields, the looming Oregon and Washington fir forests, the sun-baked deserts, the magic cities of the Pacific slope and the western ocean, the great Pacific itself.

There was the West of the settler, the rancher, the farmer and the sod-house emigrant. There was the West of the "townies," the bankers, the shopkeepers, the saloon and the brothel keepers, the sign painters, the lawyers, the church builders and the church goers, the teachers and their fledgling students.

One must include the building West, the growing and the expanding West. There were river steamers to photograph, new towns and old forts, floods and fires, disasters and natural scenic glories. All of this was new and strange, virtually unknown in the East except by the printed word and word of mouth.

A bold and busy nation, bursting with the will and energy to expand, was eagerly waiting to see all of itself through the camera lens.

And there was one other part of the West to photograph. This part was the least known. This was the part that brought fright to the trespassing settler who needed the United States Army to accompany his journey westward, to protect him, and finally to build forts along his trails for their mutual protection. This was the American Indian.

There was a great need to photograph him. The inaccurate images of the emigrant's fevered imagination were more terrifying, more immobilizing than the real live Indian. The myth of the "savage Red man" died slowly and very hard. The many drawings and paintings of artists who visited among them could not match the reality of the photograph. While artists were often perceptive to a high degree and humanistically sympathetic in their portrayals, the inherent romantic elements of contemporary painting did not provide a reassuring enough image of the Plains Indians to the westbound traveler.

Pressed unmercifully by the building railroads, the growing towns, the exploring settler and the despoiling miner; divided by bitter tribal hostilities; angered and bewildered by utterly mystifying new cultural patterns of the invading host, the American Plains Indian was fast becoming a serious problem to the American white man.

The earliest photographers in the United States, the daguerreotypists, found the Indian a valuable and often willing subject for their cameras. It is not yet possible to determine who among them may have taken the first Indian daguerreotype portrait. John Plumbe, Jr., a Washington, D.C., daguerrean artist, opened twelve galleries in American cities, including Dubuque, Iowa, and St. Louis, Missouri, in the early 1840's. In his St. Louis gallery he might easily have photographed one or more of the Indians arriving and departing regularly.

It is now believed that Josiah Gregg was making daguerreotype plates on the Santa Fe Trail as early as 1846. Possibly the drawings that illustrate his work, *The Commerce of the Prairies*, were drawn from his own daguerreotype plates.

Elmo Scott Watson, in an article for the Chicago *Westerner's Brand Book* entitled "Shadow Catchers of the Red Man," points out that J. H. Fitzgibbon, a St. Louis daguerreotypist, exhibited several Indian portraits at the 1853 Exhibition of Works of Industry at the New York Crystal Palace. Unhappily, these important plates have not been found.

Watson further notes in the same article that the Missouri Historical Society, in St. Louis, owns six slightly different daguerreotype portraits of a Sac Indian, Chief Keokuk, made in 1847 by one Thomas A. Easterly.

In a catalog of daguerreotypes exhibited in New York City early in 1851 by the celebrated San Francisco daguerrean artist Robert H. Vance, one notes "a large collection of the different tribes of Indians on the Pacific Coast."

Two additionally important daguerreotypists, John Mix Stanley and S. N. Carvalho, engage our attention for their photographs of Indians.

Elmo S. Watson writes that Dr. Robert Taft, distinguished American photographic historian, believed that Stanley was making daguerreotypes in 1843, his first venture into the West. In 1853, Stanley accompanied Governor I. I. Stevens of Washington Territory on a survey for a northern railroad route to the Pacific. On August 7, 1853 Governor Stevens records in his journal: "Mr. Stanley, the artist, was busily occupied during our stay at Fort Union with his daguerreotype apparatus and the Indians were greatly pleased with their daguerreotypes."

On September 4, 1853, Stevens writes again at Fort Benton: "Mr. Stanley commenced taking daguerreotypes of the Indians with his apparatus. They are delighted and astonished to see their likeness produced by the direct action of the sun. They worship the sun and they considered Mr. Stanley was inspired by their divinity and he thus became in their eyes a great medicine man."

S. N. Carvalho, Baltimore artist and daguerreotypist, joined the fifth exploring party of Colonel John C. Frémont at Westport, Missouri, in 1853. Traveling westward through Kansas and Colorado, Carvalho made daguerreotypes of the Cheyenne they encountered. These plates are believed to have been brought back to New York City by Colonel Frémont, and in 1856 Matthew Brady made wet-collodion glass copy negatives of them. The original daguerreotype plates, the glass copy negatives, and any paper prints from the copy negatives are believed to have been destroyed by a subsequent fire.

It is interesting to note here that these Indians, having experienced little previous contact with the white man, were unafraid and welcomed the daguerreotypists—this in spite of the understandable concern they felt about a picture-making process that was quite unintelligible to them.

But the "shadow-catchers," as the photographers were called by the Indians, soon became a real cause of concern to the latter. The original Indian attitude of skeptical cooperation soon changed into one of suspicion, mistrust, and fear. Convincing evidence of this about-face is frequently found expressed in the writings of later photographers who attempted vainly to photograph among the Indians.

As the photographic art developed, greater numbers of "shadow-catchers" came west to photograph the Indians. The distinguished American painter Albert Bierstadt, together with a colleague S. F. Frost, are reported by Captain F. W. Landers, in his report of an 1859 road survey from Salt Lake over South Pass east, as making "a set of stereoscopic views of emigrant trains, Indians, camp scenes, etc."

The troubled years during the Civil War saw a noticeable reduction in the numbers of photographers taking pictures in the West. Curiously, however, as representatives of Indian tribes proceeded to Washington, D.C., during the war years for consultations and discussions, there was a sharp increase in the formal studio portraits of such visiting delegates.

The three most important such photographers of Indian representatives were A. Z. Shindler, the well-known Matthew Brady, and the equally able and popular Alexander Gardner.

Shindler began photographing Indian delegates visiting Washington, D.C., as early as 1858. Elmo Scott Watson, in his Chicago *Brand Book* article, notes that the number of Indian portraits credited to Shindler in the "List of Photographic Portraits of Indians in the Gallery of the Smithsonian Institution" is impressive. They include, among many others, Little Crow, remembered from the Minnesota Massacre, Hold-in-the-Day

of the Chippewa, Iron Nation of the Brulé Sioux, and Struck-by-a-Bee of the Yankton Sioux. Watson is inclined to believe that these early portraits may well be the first photographs ever made of some of these famous chiefs and warriors.

As this first important listing was later incorporated into a list known as "A Descriptive Catalogue of Photographs of North American Indians," proper credit for many of these valuable Indian portraits, clearly due both Shindler and Gardner, have been omitted.

Ridgeway Glover, a young Philadelphian, was characteristic of many photographers flooding into the West with the newly-released surge of emigration after the war's end and the building of the transcontinental railroads. Glover is quoted in Watson's excellent article as saying in 1866 that he was setting out to take photographs "to illustrate the life and character of the wild men of the prairie."

Poor young Glover acknowledged taking some good pictures of the Brulé and Ogallala Sioux at Fort Laramie. In the *Philadelphia Photographer* he reported his attempts to make "instantaneous views of an Indian attack" which were denied him by the army officer in command of the threatened unit at the time. On a subsequent photographic expedition, this daring young photographer and a companion were killed on September 14, 1866, near Fort Phil Kearney, Montana Territory, by a war party of Arapaho Indians. It is reported that they cut off young Glover's head and horribly mutilated his body.

In spite of a very intense search, no trace of Glover's negatives or prints has ever been found.

Charles R. Savage, senior partner in the well-known Salt Lake City photographic firm of Savage & Ottinger, summed up the frontier photographer's problem in a report to the *Philadelphia Photographer* of his trip in 1866 across the plains from Nebraska City, Nebraska, to Salt Lake City.

"To photograph successfully on the Plains you must be perfectly safe from Indians, as on two or three occasions in our efforts to secure some views, we found ourselves alone several miles from the train and ran one or two risks of being grabbed up by a few stray rascals who are always on the lookout for a weak party and generally manage to pounce down upon a few defenceless wagons that happen to be passing. The sad fate of your former correspondent, Mr. Glover, shows how uncertain is life in such place and the wisdom of keeping a good lookout. The necessary conditions for success under such circumstances are that you must have plenty of time at your disposal, a strong party well armed with Henry rifles and good animals."

John Garbutt and T. J. Hine photographed among the Pawnee Indians in 1866, antedating William Henry Jackson's superior work among the same Indians in 1869. Alexander Gardner came west to photograph life on the Kansas frontier in the fall of 1867. In 1868 he made important and memorable photographs of several chiefs and warriors among the Crow, the Cheyenne, the Arapaho and the Sioux at the Fort Laramie peace council.

Elmo Scott Watson suggests that Spotted Tail and Swift Bear of the Brulé, Man-Afraid-of-His-Horses of the Ogallala, and Tall Mandan of the Two Kettles were photographed for the first time by Gardner at Fort Laramie. The towering Red Cloud of the Ogallala, although present at the 1868 peace council, did not then permit himself to be photographed.

In May 1870, Captain D. C. Poole of the United States 22nd Infantry and agent for the Brulé took Spotted Tail among others to Washington, D. C., for consultation. In Captain Poole's book, *Among the Sioux of Dakota,* he notes "the party refused to visit a photographer and be photograped. Spotted Tail, with all his intelligence, was Indian enough to say that he considered it bad medicine to sit for a picture, meaning that it would bring him bad luck; and whatever he said was followed by the others."

Note again the reversal in attitude on the part of Spotted Tail in the two years since he willingly posed for Alexander Gardner at Fort Laramie in 1868.

Without doubt the 1870's produced more Indian photographs of serious historic and ethnological interest than any other ten-year period. Between the professionals accompanying government survey expeditions and the numerous professional and amateur photographers flocking to open studios and galleries on the developing frontier, there were quite enough men, women, and equipment to produce this magnificent ten-year photographic legacy.

Unforgettable is the work of such Indian photographers as John K. Hillers, who accompanied the John Wesley Powell expeditions of 1871-1873, and Timothy H. O'Sullivan, who photographed widely among the Mojave, the Zuñi, the Navajo, the Coyotero Apache, the Ute and the Jicarilla Apache while photographing for several government surveys under Lieutenant George M. Wheeler.

The legendary William Henry Jackson's many negatives of the Indians are too well known to be recounted here. Other noteworthy survey photographers include William Pywell who went with General D. S. Stanley to the Yellowstone in 1873, W. H. Illingworth, who accompanied General Custer to the Black Hills in 1874, and R. Benecke, the official photographer for the Newton-Jenney Expedition into the Black Hills during 1875.

Among the many important amateur and professional frontier studio photographers were our Will Soule, Stanley J. Morrow of Yankton in the Dakota Territory, Orlando Goff of Yankton, Frank Jay Haynes of Bismarck in the Dakota Territory, and David F. Barry who had studios both at Bismarck and at Fort Bufford. Operating in the Montana Territory in this "Golden Decade" were two important photographers, L. A. Huffman, who became post photographer at Fort Keogh in 1878, and Christian Barthelmess, a soldier-photographer, many of whose original negatives wound up in Huffman's possession. Huffman undoubtedly printed and published many of Barthelmess' negatives under the Huffman imprint.

Will Soule's photographic imprint

While at Fort Keogh Huffman made the "first" portrait of the famous Sioux warrior Rain-in-the-Face, as well as Chief Crow King. The Crow, the Cheyenne, and the Sioux were among Huffman's most important Indian subjects.

Three photographers operating in the Southwest, A. Frank Randall, Ben Wittick of Santa Fe, and Camillus Fly of Tombstone, Arizona, add to the roster of the more important men photographing the American Indian through the late nineteenth century.

The Indians' attitudes, in general, toward photographers seemed to follow rather closely the general attitudes the Indians were developing toward the encroaching white man. They were forced to face the many-sided, relentless pressures of advancing settlers and builders, the puzzling and often hostile social and legal views being enforced against them by white men and their armies. Frontier photographers were often innocent victims of this disintegrating social order. Identified with the United States Army whose protection they often sought, the photographers were frequently misunderstood by the Indians. The red man's original willingness to accomodate and coexist with the whites deteriorated into hostility and bitterness which often resulted in raiding parties and guerrilla warfare of considerable effectiveness.

As sun-worshippers, bound by their own social and cultural structures, the Indians were unable to grasp the scientific reality of the work of the "shadow catchers," men able to capture "shadows," the widely accepted Indian symbol of death. The hesitancy which the Indian often felt to relinquish his image—in effect, to hand over control of some part of himself to another person—and his profound human concern in allowing his wife and children, the most defenseless of all, to be photographed, was almost always misunderstood or disregarded by the "scientific" white man.

In addition, many photographers, encouraged by their Eastern customers to produce photographs of the "good" Indian or the "sideshow" Indian, quickly lost what esteem and goodwill they may have built up among the Indian leaders, who demanded respect and understanding from their white "brothers."

With such an atmosphere in mind it is all the more surprising to view a surviving body of photographic work among the Plains Indians which reflects a certain warm trust between the participants. This is a central and challenging characteristic of the remaining prints and negatives of Will Soule's work on the Indian frontier.

Will Soule and party at an Indian camp

His portraits bespeak this trust, the views of women and children endorse it, and his scenes of tipis and camps underwrite it. It is unusual and a tribute to Soule's character that he could overcome so much suspicion and mistrust in so short a time among so many "hostile" Indians.

The lot of a photographer on the Indian frontier was a hard one. The amount of portraits one could sell to those rich enough to afford them was limited. Scenic views, while salable, had an even more limited potential in a given area. The pressing need constantly to widen one's geographical business "territory," where possible, was frequently decisive.

Even if business was always fine, the maintenance of a steady source of supplies was difficult. Shipments were not at all dependable and orders frequently incorrectly filled. Costs for materials and freight were high. There was always the opportunity for petty barter with the local tradesmen, but this did not offset the pressing need for a steady, quick return on capital invested in equipment and materials.

Overriding all of this was the necessity to refresh one's spiritual and esthetic reserves. The tedium and dreariness of frontier life was severe. For those living today an accurate description of those times and conditions seems altogether incomprehensible.

More often than not the frontier photographer doubled and tripled in brass. He or she could as well be the druggist, the stationer, the bookseller, the undertaker, or combinations of any of these. The determination to practice the photographic art on the Indian frontier, even as an amateur, was not taken lightly or accomplished easily.

Such a decision was made by William Stinson Soule (1836-1908) a Maine-born boy, 27 years old, serving the Union in a Massachusetts regiment, recovering in 1862 from a severe wound received at Antietam. Being too disabled for further active service, he spent the balance of the war working as a clerk in Washington, D.C. For a time thereafter he worked in a photographic gallery in Chambersburg, Pennsylvania. Photographic work for young Will Soule was eminently sensible as his elder brother, John P. Soule, had founded the Soule Photographic Company in Boston before the Civil War. Will's employment in the Chambersburg gallery ended when the gallery burned to the ground, completely destroying the business.

Early in 1867, Will Soule determined to "go west" to improve his shattered health. He took with him a complete outfit both for landscape photography and for portrait work under a skylight, a studio practice common at the time. Arriving at Fort Dodge in Kansas, Soule secured employment as chief clerk in the post store run by Trader John E. Tappin. It is believed that Will Soule supplemented this work with odd jobs as an amateur photographer.

Soule's first published work was an engraving, made from his photograph of a scalped hunter or sheepherder named Ralph Morrison, lying dead on the Kansas plains about a mile from Fort Dodge. This engraving was published in the January 16, 1869, issue of *Harper's Weekly*. Harper's caption indicates that "Wm. S. Soule, an amateur photographer chief clerk in Tappin's Trading Co., took the picture.... The photo was taken within an hour after the killing."

Soule appears to have remained at Fort Dodge through December, 1868. General Philip Sheridan's winter campaign against the tribes in the Indian Territory was well under way at that time. To store necessary campaign materiel, Camp Supply was established, November 18, 1868, one hundred miles to the south of Fort Dodge. That Will Soule was in Camp Supply in March of 1869 is proved by his photograph of three Cheyenne chiefs taken prisoner on the Sweetwater by Custer and the Seventh Cavalry. The picture is a clear tribute to the still defiant, even though captured, Indian warriors.

The exact dates of Will Soule's leaving Camp Supply and his arrival, permanent or temporary, at Fort Sill are still uncertain. No documentary evidence survives to fix these dates, although considerable educated guessing appears satisfactorily convincing.

There is the clear suggestion that Soule may have certainly visited Fort Sill in late 1869, returning to Camp Supply shortly thereafter. The many Soule photographs documenting the early building of Fort Sill place him there early in 1870. It seems reasonable now that Will Soule may have been formally engaged by the United States Army to make and maintain a photographic record of the building of the new fort. The rather large number of such photos by Will Soule encourages this view of his, perhaps, semi-professional status.

Earliest photos of Fort Sill construction, 1869-1870

The available evidence supports the existence of a photographic gallery at Fort Sill operated by Will Soule. It was a part of, or close to, the post trader's store run by Post Trader John S. Evans.

The fact that Fort Sill was, from its inception, both the Indian Agency and the Military Control Headquarters for the Comanche, the Kiowa, the Kiowa-Apache, the Wichita, the Caddo and other tribes lends strong support to the belief that most of the surviving Indian portraits were taken at or near Fort Sill between 1870 and 1875. It is believed that late in the fall of 1874 or early in 1875 Will Soule left the Indian Territory for his home in Boston.

John P. Soule, Will's elder brother, copyrighted many of the Fort Sill Indian photographs through the Library of Congress sometime in

1873. As late as 1891, Will Soule, then in his Boston studio, was offering "to fill orders for photographs of Indian celebrities at No. 363 Washington Street."

Returning to the photographic business in Boston in partnership with W. D. Everett, Soule soon married, left the business in 1902, and died in the summer of 1908 in the midst of preparations for a European trip. He was survived by his wife and the elder of two daughters, Lucia A. Soule.

Of Will Soule's work on the Indian frontier, 166 paper prints and sixty-nine original glass plate negatives are known to have survived. They are represented in various collections from the Bureau of American Ethnology through the Fort Sill Artillery and Missile Center Museum, the Denver Public Library, the Huntington Library, and the Los Angeles County Museum of Natural History.

A survey of the known materials clearly indicate Soule's photographs to have included other than Indian portraits and views of Indian life. Some photographs of garrison life at Fort Sill, the early construction of the fort, portraits of some white army scouts and interpreters are all included. The likely range of Soule's interest suggests that only a small fragment of his eight years of work on the Indian frontier may have survived.

Missing from his remaining work are photographs of day-to-day events he would normally have wished to "cover." The variety of cavalry expeditions on escort duty at the fort, changes of station, patrols against Indians and outlaws, the full scope of an active cavalry unit at a busy

Post Trader John S. Evan's store at Fort Sill

frontier post would hardly have been overlooked by a photographer. What of the many portraits of soldiers and officers on duty at the post, as well as of their wives and children? Where are they?

Will Soule, or any photographer present, would not have missed General Sherman's visit to Fort Sill in 1871 where, in consultation with Kiowa chiefs on General Grierson's front porch, Sherman narrowly escaped assassination by the Indians. The arrival at Fort Sill of MacKenzie and the Fourth Cavalry to take imprisoned Indian chiefs back to Texas to stand trial should be among Will Soule's photographs. Where was Will Soule and his camera at the October 1873 conference at Fort Sill between Governor Davis of Texas, the Commissioner of Indian Affairs and the Superintendent of the Plains Tribes with Comanche, Kiowa, and other Indian tribes? This important conference lasted several days, attracted thousands of Indians, the garrison was under arms, long speeches were made by the principal Indian chiefs, correspondents from important Eastern periodicals were in attendance, and national interest in the proceedings was high. If Will Soule were present he would surely have photographed such an event, wouldn't he?

Perhaps the question more to the point is to acknowledge that he did and ask where are the prints or the negatives?

Finally, in August 1874, Fort Sill was the operational center for the last of the army campaigns against the Southern Plains tribes. Hundreds of friendly Indians were soon at the post, and succeeding weeks saw many groups of "hostiles" coming in for surrender. The final dramatic scenes of "pacification" were being played out at Fort Sill. We are still uncertain about whether Will Soule had already left for the East in this fall of 1874. It is the only reason he would not have recorded this with his camera and his glass plates.

It is possible, although this writer considers it doubtful, that Will Soule was essentially a studio portrait photographer and remained indifferent to the surging and vigorous life surrounding him in and at the fort. What remains of his work is invaluable. Any search for the balance of his undiscovered photographic work on the Indian frontier would, if successful, add immeasurably to our national historic heritage.

For many years those persons interested in Will Soule's frontier photographs believed that his original wet-plate collodion glass plate negatives were either irretrievably lost or carelessly destroyed over the years. The author held the same view until research into the life and work of another early American photographer suggested a clue to the location of the missing Soule negatives.

Lawrie Tatum, Quaker Indian agent at Fort Sill

On reading copies of some of Henry Peabody's extensive correspondence, the author noted mention by Peabody of the Soule negatives. Henry G. Peabody, an important professional photographer, first made the acquaintance of Will Soule in Boston early in 1886. Soule was at that time the senior partner, in partnership with W. D. Everett, of the Soule Photographic Company of Boston. Peabody maintained a close business and professional relationship with Will Soule for fifteen years, seeing him almost every day. They appear to have enjoyed each other as friends, including each other's family as time allowed. Selling out his business interests to W. D. Everett, Will Soule retired in 1902 and died in the summer of 1908. His younger daughter had died a few years previously, and his wife lingered on only a few years after his death. Will Soule's older daughter Lucia A. Soule lived on for many years.

Some years after Will Soule's death, Lucia Soule shipped all of her father's Indian negatives that she could find to Mr. Peabody in California. Although the number is not accurately specified, it would seem to be close to a total of seventy-five. She asked Mr. Peabody to print a small group of the negatives and deposit the prints with the Bureau of American Ethnology in Washington, D.C. Peabody did so, indicating that he *did not* print the remaining balance of the negatives. After some years, Mr. Peabody gave or sold the Soule negatives to the Audio-Visual Section of the Los Angeles County Board of Education. The use of projected photographic prints in classrooms for educational purposes was then beginning to be popular.

Armed with this lead, the author was able successfully to locate the long-missing negatives. In time, they were physically transferred to the Los Angeles County Museum of Natural History. They are presently in the direct custody of the History Division at the County Museum.

Of the approximately seventy-five plates sent by Miss Soule to Mr. Peabody, some six are lost or so badly broken they were thrown away. The collection today consists of sixty-nine printable plates, some few of which are broken. None is severely damaged. Storage over the years and careless carriage have accounted for the losses mentioned above. They seem to have been individually handled with commendable care. Most of the plates were jacketed and bore some identification. The notations are believed to be in Will Soule's hand and, in the main, are phonetic spellings of the Indian names. Not all of the plates are so identified, and often a plate may simply refer to "Wichita Woman" or "Cheyenne Warrior." No further identification in such cases is noted on the plates or jackets.

Further useful identification has been possible through the work of the Bureau of American Ethnology, the carefully thorough and tireless research of Gillet Griswold, Director of the United States Army Artillery and Missile Center Museum at Fort Sill, Lawton, Oklahoma, and finally Colonel Wilbur S. Nye who is currently preparing an extensive biographical study of William S. Soule. The authors of this book are deep in obligation to the last two named men.

They have shared hard-won knowledge and important research conclusions with open-handed generosity and trust. William S. Soule's work deserves very serious attention by photographers, historians, and ethnologists. It is hoped it will compel admiration and appreciation from the general public as well.

For the "Golden Ten Years" of the 1870's we do not yet have enough photographs of the Southern Plains tribes, the vaunted "Lords of the Plains." Soule's remaining work may represent the single largest body now known of such photographs, compressed into the brief time period in which he worked.

These few years were critical ones in the United States Government's long attempts to "pacify" these hostile Indians. The chiefs and warriors shown in these photographs were then free, proud braves, confident still of their ability to live on, in the old ways, on their own lands.

These are the Indians whom the white men justly feared. The portraits are not of pacified, over-dressed, "carnival" Indians with whom the white man could feel comfortable. These were warriors in every sense of the word, able and deadly. Such Indians could endure hardships beyond belief, ride like mounted demons, and fight with indescribable fury. These Comanche, Kiowa, Kiowa-Apache, Arapaho, Apache were the "savage" defenders of their families, their homes, their tribal rights, and their traditional tribal lands.

These are the Indians who died fighting the white man, not those who surrendered to be imprisoned and to die on government reservations. The names of many of these warriors are still uttered with pride by their living descendants.

It speaks much of Will Soule as a man that he was able to enjoy the limited trust and confidence of such warriors. It was this trust and confidence that enabled him to make the portraits of them that we can see again today. Such portraits and views should help us understand more clearly the tragic and bloody relationships created between American Indians and the white majority over two hundred difficult years of technological progress.

KIOWA
KIOWA-APACHE
AND
PLAINS CULTURE

For the American Indian, the Plains culture was the last to evolve in North America. It was a complex of many tribes of varied ancestry, language and culture, developed completely within the period of white penetration into the Americas. It was a culture which, ironically, depended upon an animal brought by the 17th century Spanish as they moved into Texas, New Mexico and California—the horse; for the Plains were not really habitable until its chief food source, buffalo, could be successfully hunted.

Of the thirty-one Plains tribes, who for most of us symbolize the American Indian, twenty were "marginal"; that is they stuck to river valleys, lived in villages and kept up their horticulture and sedentary arts, while at the same time adopting the horse. Both the Caddo and Wichita are representative of this group. The remaining eleven tribes, including the Kiowa, Kiowa-Apache, Comanche, Arapaho and Cheyenne, became horsemen and gave the Plains culture its name.

Some say the horse made the Plains Indian a new man, psychically as well as physically. It certainly gave him wealth and prestige. It made him not just a hunter but a warrior and a dangerous predator. As the whole area of the Plains now opened up to men and horses, a new per-

sonality arose. It was the "centaur," now master of his environment—one which had long frustrated his efforts to conquer it. With the leisure afforded by riding, his mentality opened to new interests, including war and wealth, trade, magic and religion. The horse made the Plains Indian independent of his environment; and, except for a few friendly confederates, he was antisocial. His early predatory activities were directed mainly against the Spanish, Mexicans and Texans. Later their soldier societies (warrior) were called upon to defend territory, first against the white settlers moving west, then, finally, against the United States Army. But the glamour and pageantry of Plains Indian life had within it the seeds of its own destruction and his culture ended as it had begun—with the dependence on the horse. First the buffalo and then the horse was taken away. By 1880 the "centaur" personality was gone; and with it went the spirit of the Plains Indian.

Both the Kiowa and Kiowa-Apache were typical Plains tribes. But they were not always so. The earliest inhabitants of the Great Plains area were Athabascan-speaking peoples—Apaches. They ranged from present west Texas up the Plains, at least as far north as the Platte, and probably into Canada. They were met by the first Spanish expeditions eastward from the upper Rio Grande and throughout the 17th century dominated much of the western Plains. About 1700 the Shoshonean-speaking Comanche began to change from a mountain-based culture to a nomadic Plains life, taking over the horse and steadily expanding their range at the expense of the Apache. By the middle of the 18th century, they swept the latter from the Plains north of the Canadian and, by 1800 the Comanche shared the upper Arkansas valley and territory to the north with the Kiowa, Arapaho, Cheyenne and others.

The historic traditions of the Kiowas place them at the Yellowstone and Missouri rivers in what is now western Montana. With the Flatheads as their neighbors, the Kiowas were a hunting people, dependent on the bow and arrow for small game, apparently knowing nothing of the buffalo. About 1650, according to legend, a tribal disagreement caused one group to move out of the mountains to the southeast. In the Black Hills they met the Crow, with whom they made a permanent alliance about 1700. Living with the Kiowa in the Black Hills was the tribe they brought with them from their former home in the mountains, the small tribe of Athabascans called the Kiowa-Apache. Although speaking a different language, the Kiowa-Apaches resembled the Kiowas in customs, dress and general character. Observers have noted, however, that the former were more agreeable, reliable and peaceful. This was due in part, perhaps, to Pacer, their chief of many years. He had considerable ability and was a consistent advocate of peace with the white man. On the whole, the Kiowa-Apaches seemed a quieter and less ambitious group than the Kiowas.

By about 1765, the Kiowas had adopted most of the Crow (i.e. Plains) culture: the horse and buffalo-skin tipi, the Sun Dance, the lance and the Indian soldier societies. From then to 1837, the time of their first treaty with the United States, was their Golden Age. For many years they lived in peace with the many tribes of present South Dakota: Arikaras, Pawnees, Hidatsas, Crows and Mandans. These were all for the most part sedentary agricultural groups, who, unlike the Kiowa, would not exploit their horse culture to the fullest. About 1775, the Dakotas drove the Kiowas and their southern neighbors, the Comanches, southward into the area of the upper Arkansas. A few years later both groups made peace and, although different in language and temperament, a Comanche-Kiowa alliance was made permanent. They, with the Kiowa-Apaches, now held the territory of the southern Great Plains in common, driving the indigenous Mescalero and Lipan Apaches into New Mexico and Old Mexico. To the northeast they pushed back the Wichita confederation and in Texas the Tonkawa confederation, taking from them their joint hunting grounds. Raiding and trading became profitable businesses and the Kiowas raided far south and west, from Texas to Sonora to the Gulf of California. They were frequently at war with the Cheyennes, Dakota, Pawnee, Caddos and Navahos.

By 1834 most of their enemies had made a grudging peace and the confederated Kiowas, Kiowa-Apaches and Comanches ruled the territory they had pre-empted. The historic treaty with the Cheyennes and Arapahos in 1840 joined five major tribes with a total population of nearly 16,000.

The year 1849 not only brought thousands of Americans to California; it also brought cholera to the Kiowas and nearly half of them perished. It was the year that the Kiowas would turn their fury on the white settlers and eventually the United States Army.

For the next twenty-five years, almost to the month (December, 1874), the Kiowas and their allies fought many battles, signed many treaties, suffered many depravations; and in the end it was not so much the body but the spirit which collapsed. Satanta, a Kiowa chief, once said that "he took hold of that part of the white man's road that was represented by the breech-loading gun, but did not like the ration of corn; it hurt (my) teeth. The good Indian, he that listens to the white man, got nothing. The independent Indian was the only one that was rewarded." In the end neither Indian won.

Additional information on those photographs marked with an asterisk may be found on pages 58-60. The individuals in this group are Kiowa unless otherwise indicated.

Sitting Bear (Satank, Set-angya) *

White Horse (Tsen-tainte)*

Big Bow (Zepko-eete)*

Kicking Bird (Striking Eagle, T'ene-angopte)*

Woman Heart (Woman's Heart, Manyi-ten)*

White Bear (Satanta)*

White Bear (Satanta)*

Cry of the Wild Goose (Sa-lo-so, Tsa'l-au-te)*

Brave in War Dress

Brave in War Dress (probably Koi-khan-hole)

Brave in War Dress

Big Tree (A'do-eette)*

Big Tree's sister

Pacer (Peso, Essa-queta): Kiowa-Apache*

Pacer's Son: Kiowa-Apache

Brave: Kiowa-Apache

Black Hawk: Kiowa-Apache

Lone Wolf (Guipago)*

Sitting-in-the-Saddle (Tau-ankia, Tibone): Lone Wolf's son*

Sitting-in-the-Saddle: another view*

Two Braves: Kiowa-Apache

Lone Bear (Tar-lo): dressed as a Kiowa boy

Lone Bear (Tar-lo): dressed as an Osage boy

Trotting Wolf (Gu-ee-ah-pay, Coyote Walking) and Squaw

Tom-e-ath-to (Trailing the Enemy, Eonah-pah) and Squaw (probably the eldest daughter of Satanta)*

Two Squaws

Two Squaws

Standing Sweat-House (Tape-day-ah)*

Sah-tope-ay-doh: Satanta's youngest daughter. Her hair is cut, perhaps in mourning for her father's imprisonment in Texas.

Two Squaws (*on left*: Sah-tope-ay-doh, Pipe-holder, Holds-the-pipe: youngest daughter of Satanta; *on right*: Big Tree's sister)

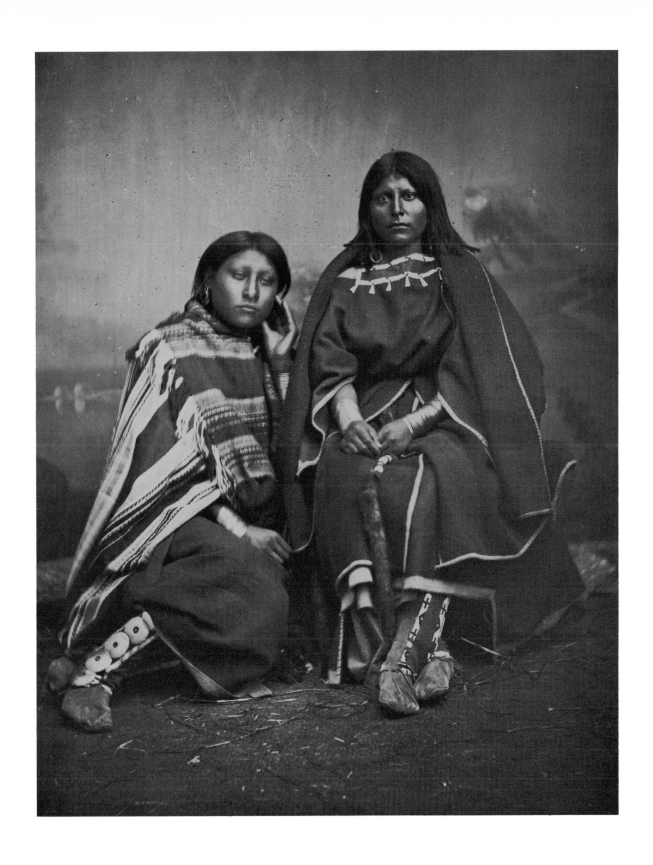

Two Squaws

Stumbling Bear (Set-imkia)*

Son of the Sun (Sun Boy, Pai-talyi)*

Kiowa camp near the Canadian River, 1869. Kicking Bird died here in 1875

Five Braves. *Left to right*: Poor Buffalo (Haw-taudle); Short Greasy Hair
(Odl-Kaun't-say-hah); Buffalo Chap (Hair Portion of Leg, Kaw-tom-te);
Never Got Shot (Haun-goon-pau); Feather Head (A'tah-ladte)

NOTES ON THE PHOTOGRAPHS

Pacer (Peso, Essa-queta)

Pacer, Chief of the Kiowa-Apaches for many years, was a man of considerable intelligence and ability and was a consistent advocate of peace. On August 19, 1873, two Indian prisoners, Satanta and Big Tree, were sent from Huntsville prison, Texas, to Fort Sill. A council was held on October 6, in front of Colonel Davidson's headquarters, to present the various Indian groups with the terms for the release of the two prisoners. Pacer was at this conference along with Governor Davis (Texas); E. P. Smith, Commissioner of Indian Affairs; Enoch Hoag, Superintendent of the Plains tribes; Satanta's son, Cry of the Wild Goose; Lone Wolf; Kicking Bird; Horseback; Esa-ton-yett, and others. Among the many who made speeches was Pacer: "... Tell the Governor of Texas we are about to take a new road, and throw the old one away ... I have worked hard to keep the peace and will work still harder ... We are (Indian) men, but our children will be white men. Build us houses and teach our children to read and write, but above all release Satanta and Big Tree...."

Pacer had long sought for the building of a school for his people. In 1875, the year of his death, one was established by A. J. Standing, a Quaker. Pacer is buried in the Post Cemetery at Fort Sill.

Kicking Bird (Striking Eagle, T'ene-angopte)

Kicking Bird has been described as "... a remarkable man, slight in form compared with the burly warriors of his tribe, but tall, sinewy, agile and very graceful. His extremely affable bearing gave him command among his own people ... If he had been white he would have been a United States senator."

Kicking Bird was one of the signers of the Medicine Lodge Treaty (1867); and he may have been the only Chief present who was willing to follow the treaty's terms. The ceremony was almost broken up by his unusual attire—a breach cloth and a high black silk hat obtained earlier from United States Commissioner Alf Taylor. A year later Kicking Bird and Woman's Heart led a small band of Kiowas away from the Fort Cobb agency to the Staked Plains. Here they joined the Kwahadis and later joined with Lone Wolf and White Horse in pleading for the release of Satanta and Big Tree.

Kicking Bird's last raid was in 1870 when he led a hundred warriors south across the Red River. He had made this expedition because he had been accused of cowardice and for consorting too much with the white man at Fort Sill. He later expressed regret for the war party (which was successful) and afterwards devoted himself to promoting peaceful relations with the authorities.

Kicking Bird was influential in persuading his people to surrender at Fort Sill, January 1875. In selecting the prisoners to be sent to Florida, including White Horse, Woman's Heart and Lone Wolf, he said: "I long ago took the white man by the hand; I have never let it go.... I have worked hard to bring my people on the white man's road ... This country was given by Washington to his red children. I now see white men in it, making lines.... We do not know what it means, but we are afraid that it is not for our good. The white man is strong, but he cannot destroy us all in one year ... maybe four years and then the world will turn to water ... it is our mother, and cannot live when the Indians are all dead."

As a result of his peaceful attitude, Kicking Bird made powerful enemies among the war chiefs of the tribe; and he was to suffer martyrdom, dying on May 4, 1875, probably of poison.

Big Tree (A'do-eette)

Chief Big Tree, only twenty-three years of age, won renown in Heap-of-Bears' Texas raid of 1868. He was described by Captain Robert Carter: "(compared to Santanta) (he) was much lighter in color, smaller in stature, and much inferior in his general appearance.... There was something in his face ... that betokened the crafty sneak, and he lacked nobility of manner and expression."

Big Tree planned an unsuccessful raid on Fort Sill in 1870 and in the following year he (with Satanta and Satank) participated in the Warren Wagon Train Massacre near Jacksboro, Texas. When the Kiowa chiefs bragged at Fort Sill of their exploit, they were arrested at a dramatic confrontation with General William Tecumseh Sherman at the Fort. Sent to Texas for an unprecedented civil trial, Santanta and Big Tree were sentenced to death. (Satank was shot and killed while trying to escape en route to the trial.) District Attorney Lanham, in his closing summation to the jury, referred to Big Tree by saying: "In Big Tree we perceive the tiger-demon who tasted blood and loved it ... who stops at no crime how black so ever ... he can scalp, burn ... and deface his victims, with all the superlatives of cruelty and have no feeling of sympathy or remorse."

Both Big Tree and Satanta were released in 1873, when the Kiowas and Comanches threatened the United States with retaliatory raids. Briefly confined again in 1875, this time at Fort Sill, Big Tree was soon released to settle on the reservation. He became a Christian convert and for some thirty years he served as a deacon in the Rainy Mountain Indian Mission Church. Big Tree died in 1930.

Big Bow (Zepko-eete)

Thomas Battey, minister and teacher who lived with the Kiowas wrote: "Big Bow . . . has probably killed and scalped more white people than any other living Kiowa; and (with White Horse) has been for years the terror of the frontiers, not only of Texas, but of Kansas, Colorado, and New Mexico . . . prowling about in secret, seeking whom they might destroy . . . (he has) a more treacherous and ferocious countenance than when I last saw him . . . not likely to atone for the evil they have done. . . ."

Big Bow had refused to participate in the Medicine Lodge Council. He was with Big Tree at the Warren Wagon Train Massacre and led, in 1872, another attack on a wagon train at Howard Wells. Until 1875, he had escaped capture. In January of that year, and with the help of Kicking Bird, Colonel Davidson promised Big Bow that he would not be punished if he brought his people into Fort Sill. Big Bow was then sent out to bring in Lone Wolf, and the reign of the Kiowas was over.

Sitting Bear (Satank, Set-angya)

Satank, born in the Black Hills (South Dakota) about 1815, was a Kiowa Chief and medicine-man. He became prominent at an early age and is credited with having been a principal agent in negotiating the historic peace treaty, in 1840, of five Indian tribes: Comanche, Kiowa, Kiowa-Apache, Cheyenne, and Arapaho. This treaty, never broken, joined together these tribes who would act to form a barrier to the westward-pushing Indians and to the encroaching whites, especially the Texans. Later, Satank participated in and headed the list of signers of the Medicine Lodge Treaty of 1867.

In 1870, Satank's son was killed while raiding in Texas. Arriving at the scene to recover the remains, Satank found only a heap of bones. When the Chief saw what was left of his beloved son, his friends had to tie him with a lariat to prevent him from committing suicide. They allowed him to gather the bones, wash them, and bundle them in a new blanket. Satank carried these bones with him wherever he went; and it became a familiar sight in the Kiowa tribe to see the chief riding along in sorrow, leading a gentle horse laden with the remains of his son. Satank was often described as having the habitual expression of a man who had just swallowed a big dose of quinine. This was perhaps due, in part, to his mustache which he used to hide a scar on his upper lip (from an old arrow wound).

Satank was arrested at Fort Sill in 1871 for his part in the Warren Wagon Train Massacre. On the way to Texas to stand trial for the teamsters' killing, with Lone Wolf, Big Tree and White Bear, Satank deliberately invited his death. Singing the death song of the soldier society, he slipped off his handcuffs, drew a concealed knife and sprang at a guard. Satank died quickly in a hail of bullets.

White Bear (Satanta)

Born about 1807, Satanta was recognized as second chief of the Kiowas. The first rank was his senior, Satank, and later Lone Wolf, although probably neither of these equaled him in force and ability. His eloquence in council gained for him the title of "Orator of the Plains"; his boldness, directness and his keen sense of humor made him a favorite with some army officers and peace commissioners despite his known hostility to them.

In 1866, at Fort Dodge, Satanta met General W. S. Hancock to complain about the Indian agent Jesse Leavenworth. Hancock was so impressed with Satanta that he presented him with a new uniform of a major general. The chief could not wait to have his picture taken in his new outfit. Later Henry M. Stanley, correspondent of the New York *Tribune* wrote: ". . . He has won a great name for reckless daring all the way from the Arkansas to the Rio Grande. His name is on every lip and his praises are sounded by the young damsels of his tribe as the greatest chief and warrior of the red man. His figure is large and very muscular. As he stood in the council, his sharp brilliant eyes wandered incessantly around the circle." It was said also that Satanta was brazen, impudent and addicted to violence and boasting.

Satanta was the second signator to the Medicine Lodge Treaty of 1867, although he probably had no intention of obeying the provisions. "I do not want to settle down in the houses you would build for us. I love to roam over the wild prairie. There I am free and happy."

For boastfully admitting his part in the Texas wagon train fight in 1871, Satanta (with Sitting Bear and Big Tree) was arrested. In July of that year the historic trial of Satanta and Big Tree was held at Jacksboro, Texas. The prosecuting attorney, Samuel W. T. Lanham, later Governor of Texas, addressed the jury: ". . . we recognize in Satanta the arch fiend of treachery and blood, the cunning Cataline, the promoter of strife, the breaker of treaties signed by his own hand, the inciter of his fellows to rapine and murder, the artful dealer in bravado while in the powwow, and the most abject coward in the field, as well as the most canting and double-tongued hypocrite where detected and overcome. . . ."

Although Lanham's oratory convinced the jury to vote the death sentence for Satanta and Big Tree, it was later commuted to life imprisonment. Released in 1873, Satanta was re-arrested in 1874. Two years later he committed suicide by throwing himself from an upper story of the prison hospital.

Sitting-in-the-Saddle (Tau-ankia, Tibone)

Tau-ankia, Lone Wolf's favorite son, had taken part in the attack on a wagon train at Howard Wells, Texas, April 20, 1872. Seventeen teamsters were killed in this raid; Tau-ankia was wounded in the leg. Shortly after at a Fort Sill conference (1873), at which the Indians promised to "take up the white man's road and to cease raiding" (in return for the release of Satanta and Big Tree), a number of Comanches and Kiowas went south after horses and scalps. United States troops caught the marauding band at South Kickapoo Spring, Texas, December 7, 1873. One of the leaders, Tau-ankia, limping badly from his previous injury, was shot and killed.

Cry of the Wild Goose (Sa-lo-so, Tsa'l-au-te)

Sa-lo-so was present when his father Satanta, and Lone Wolf, were taken hostage by General Sheridan and Colonel Custer (1868), as United States troops attempted to move the various tribes to Fort Cobb. Sa-lo-so later became a member of the Indian police.

Lone Wolf (Guipago)

Lone Wolf, a Kiowa chief, was one of the nine signers of the treaty of Medicine Lodge. After the 1871 Texas wagon train raid, Lone Wolf escaped General William T. Sherman's trap at Fort Sill, in which White Bear, Sitting Bear and Big Tree were captured. A year later Lone Wolf had become the recognized leader of the Kiowas following their tribal Sun Dance on the Red River. Following the surrender of the Kiowas in the spring of 1875, Lone Wolf, with a number of others, was sent to military confinement at Fort Marion, Florida. He died in 1879, shortly after his return to the reservation in Oklahoma.

Standing Sweat-House (Tape-day-ah)

Tape-day-ah was one of the nine Kiowas and twenty-one Comanches who raided in Texas after the Fort Sill conference, October 1873. He also participated in a war party recruited by Lone Wolf for a revenge raid on Texas, 1874. The following year Tape-day-ah was one of a group of Army scouts organized by Kicking Bird sent to persuade the Kiowas to surrender.

Tom-e-ath-to (Trailing the Enemy, Eonah-pah) and Squaw (probably the eldest daughter of Satanta)

Eonah-pah was the only Kiowa who actively participated in the Battle of the Washita, November 27, 1868. Here Eonah-pah helped many to escape Colonel Custer's raid on Black Kettle's Cheyenne camp. In 1873-74 he was with Tape-day-ah in the raids on Texas. Several years later Eonah-pah became an Army scout.

White Horse (Tsen-tainte)

White Horse was one of the outstanding warriors of his tribe. He led the "raid on the mules at Fort Sill (1870), and was one of the group who attacked Adobe Walls, Texas. White Horse surrendered in December, 1874, and was sent to Fort Marion, Florida, for confinement. He was returned to Fort Sill in 1878.

Woman Heart (Woman's Heart, Manyi-ten)

As one of the Kiowa chiefs, Woman Heart was with an Indian delegation to Washington, D.C., 1872. Jailed with White Horse and Big Tree in 1875, Woman Heart was later sent to a Florida prison.

Son of the Sun (Sun Boy, Pai-talyi)

Chief Sun Boy is shown here in a coat borrowed from Major General Winfield Scott Hancock. The occasion was probably the Medicine Lodge Creek Treaty conference in 1867. In 1872 Sun Boy was a member of a delegation of Kiowa Indians selected by the government to visit Washington, D.C. It was hoped that the Indians "would develop some appreciation of the power and the threats of the government." On the way the delegation met briefly with Satanta and Big Tree at the Everette House in St. Louis. The latter two, sentenced to life imprisonment, had been brought from Texas for this special meeting. In Washington the Commissioner of Indian Affairs promised the delegation that he would release Satanta and Big Tree if they would stop raiding.

In the fall of 1877 Chief Sun Boy was one of the ten prominent chiefs who received a government built six-hundred dollar house at Fort Sill.

Stumbling Bear (Set-imkia)

Although Chief Stumbling Bear was always known for his peaceful attitude, he had become one of the heroes in the successful defense of a Kiowa camp attacked by a large force of cavalrymen commanded by Colonel Christopher (Kit) Carson, 1864. Stumbling Bear, with Kicking Bird, usually represented the peaceful elements of the Kiowas and both were present at the Treaty of Medicine Lodge in 1867. He was one of the delegates sent to Washington, D.C. in 1872 and, in 1876, Stumbling Bear received one of the houses at Fort Sill, built especially for a number of prominent Indian chiefs.

CADDO AND WICHITA

According to tribal traditions the lower Red River of Louisiana was the early home of the Caddo. Cabeza de Vaca and his companions in 1525-36 crossed a portion of the territory occupied by the Caddo, and De Soto's expedition encountered some of the tribes of the Caddo confederacy in 1540-41; but the Indians did not become known until they were met by La Salle and his followers in 1687. At that time the Caddo villages were scattered along the Red River and its tributaries in what are now Louisiana and Arkansas and East Texas. The Caddo were not the only occupants of this wide territory; other Indian confederacies belonging to the same linguistic family also resided there. These various tribes and confederacies were alternately allies and enemies of the Caddo.

The native population was so divided that at no time could it successfully resist the white settlers. At an early date the Caddo obtained horses from the Spaniards through intermediate tribes; they learned to rear these animals and traded with them as far north as Illinois. During the 18th century, wars in Europe led to contention between the Spaniards and the French for the territory occupied by the Caddo. The brunt of these contentions fell upon the Indians; the trails between their villages became routes for armed forces, while the villages were transformed into garrisoned posts. The Caddo were friendly to the French and rendered valuable service, but they suffered greatly from contact with the whites. Tribal wars were fomented, villages were abandoned, new diseases spread havoc among the people, and by the close of the century the welcoming attitude of the Indians during its early years had changed to one of defense and distrust. Several tribes were practically extinct, others seriously reduced in numbers and a once thrifty and numerous people had become demoralized and were more or less wanderers in their native land.

With the acquisition of Louisiana by the United States, white immigration increased and the Caddo were pushed from their old haunts. Under their first treaty, with the United States, in 1835, they ceded all their land and agreed to move at their own expense beyond the boundaries of the United States, never to return and settle as a tribe. The tribes living in Louisiana, being thus forced to leave their old home, moved toward Texas. At that time the Texans were contending with Mexico for independence, and no tribe could live at peace with both the opposing forces. Public opinion was divided as to the treatment of the Indians; one party demanded a policy of extermination, the other advocated conciliatory methods.

In 1843 the governor of the Republic of Texas sent a commission to the tribes to fix a line between them and the white settlers and to establish three trading posts; but as the land laws of the Texas Republic did not recognize the Indian's rights of occupance, there was no power which could successfully prevent a white settler from taking land that had been cultivated by an Indian. This condition led to continual difficulties, and these did not diminish after the annexation of Texas to the United States, as Texas retained control and jurisdiction over all its public domain. The fields of peaceable Indians were often taken and the natives were hunted down and killed. The more warlike tribes resorted to reprisals, and bitter feelings were common. Immigration increased and the inroads on the buffalo herds by the newcomers made the food of the Indians scarce. Appeals were sent to the Federal Government and in 1855 a tract near the Brazos River was secured and a number of Caddo and other Indians were induced to colonize under the supervision of Agent Robert S. Neighbours. The Indians built houses, tilled fields, raised cattle, sent their children to school, living quiet, orderly lives.

The Comanche to the west continued to raid upon the settlers, some of whom turned indiscriminately upon all Indians. The Caddo were the chief sufferers in these reprisals, although they helped the state troops to bring the Comanche raiders to justice. In 1859 a company of white settlers fixed a date for the massacre of all the reservation Indians. The Caddos appealed to the Federal Government for help and through the strenuous efforts of Agent Neighbours the Caddo made a forced march for fifteen days in torrid July heat; men, women, and children (with the loss of more than half of their stock and possessions) safely reached the banks of the Washita River in Oklahoma where a reservation was set apart for them. During the Civil War the Caddo remained loyal to the Union while taking refuge in Kansas and as far west as Colorado. In 1872 the boundaries of their reservation were re-defined, and in 1902 every man, woman, and child received an allotment of land under the provisions of the severalty act of 1887, by which they became citizens of the United States and subject to the laws of Oklahoma. In 1904 the Caddos numbered 535 souls.

The other tribes of the Caddoan family include the Arikara in North Dakota, Middle Pawnee of Nebraska and the Wichita. As with all of the Caddoan tribes the Wichita were primarily sedentary and agricultural although, of course, they also hunted the buffalo. Their permanent communal houses were conical in shape, from 30 to 50 feet in diameter, and consisted of a framework of stout poles overlaid with grass thatch. The completed structure was about fifteen feet high and was shaped like a beehive. The Wichita raised large quantities of corn, pumpkins and tobacco, trading the surplus to the neighboring hunting tribes. The Wichita were generally known as an industrious, reliable people of friendly disposition.

The name Wichita is of uncertain origin.

They have been known variously as Tattooed Faces, to the Kiowa and Comanche, and Black Pawnee to the Sioux. The first people definitely known to have lived for any length of time at the present site of Fort Sill were the Wichitas. The first historical mention of this group is in 1541, when the Spanish explorer Coronado entered the territory known to his New Mexican Indian guides as the country of Quivira. He found them living in villages of distinctive grass houses located in what is now central Kansas. In the next two centuries the Wichita were gradually forced westward and south by the Osage, Pawnee and Chickasaw. By the mid-1700's they had settled at the site of Spanish Fort, Texas, on the Red River. In 1801 the Wichita lost nearly one-half of their tribe when smallpox ravaged a number of the Texas tribes.

From 1825 to 1842 many Eastern immigrant Indians had been escorted by the United States Army to new land west of the Mississippi. Prominent among these immigrants were the Five Civilized Tribes—Creek, Cherokee, Choctaw, Chickasaw and Seminole—who settled in what is now eastern Oklahoma. They had lived in the southeastern United States and shared among themselves a similar culture and history. They had already decided to pattern themselves after the white man, and in fact they came to resemble him very much in economic, political and social forms. These tribes soon found themselves at odds with their Indian neighbors over landownership. To prevent open warfare a chain of forts from Minnesota to Louisiana was constructed to guard the "Permanent Indian Frontier." But in 1834 the natives of the Indian Country, including the Wichitas, made war upon their new unwelcome neighbors. A peace treaty the following year failed to pacify the Plains Indians and it was not until the 1840's that the Five Civilized Tribes came to enjoy reasonably amicable relations with the nomads.

There was now a much more serious threat posed to the Wichitas, Kiowas, Comanches and Cheyennes. It was the pressure of the white advance. Following the treaty of 1835, the Wichitas moved to the present site of Fort Sill where they remained until 1850, when malaria and lack of game forced a move to Rush Springs, about thirty miles away. The next seventeen years brought additional demoralization and suffering and by 1867 the Wichita had lost nearly eighty percent of their people by disease and hardship. In that year they and allied tribes were finally assigned a reservation on the north side of the Washita River, in what is now Caddo County, Oklahoma. In 1902 they were given allotments in severalty and the reservation was thrown open to settlement.

Caddo George Washington

Caddo George had a "store" near Anadarko and he "bootlegged arms and whiskey to the Kiowas and Comanches while posing as a firm friend of the authorities." He was present as an observer when Satanta, Big Tree and Satank were sent, in irons, to Texas for trial. As the wagons left Fort Sill, Satank called to Caddo George: "Take this message to my people. Tell them I died beside the road. My bones will be found there. Tell my people to gather them up and carry them away. Tell the Kiowas to bring back the mules and don't raid more. Do as the agent tells them."

Caddo George Washington

Caddo Village

Heap Wolves (*probably* Esa-dowa). Killed by Osaga in 1872

Squaw

Nawatry

Squaw

Two Squaws

Three Squaws (*left to right*: Nawatry, Dudu, Ske-zitz)

Squaw

CHEYENNE

The Cheyenne (or Tsistsistas, meaning The People) were one of the most notable of the western tribes inhabiting the Great Plains, the open country lying west of the Mississippi River and east of the Rocky Mountains. They were famous among early travelers for the chastity of their women and the courage of their warriors; in later years, when everything was in change, the Cheyenne were considered the most conservative of the Plains Indians. Their attitudes toward sex and war, and toward the maintenance of their social order are outstanding features of their way of life. Several hundred years ago, the Cheyenne resided in the woodland country of the western Great Lakes (probably in the vicinity of Lake Superior). Toward the end of the 17th century they migrated westward, settling on the Red River where it forms the border between Minnesota and the Dakotas. Early in the 18th century they became closely associated with the sedentary village tribes of the upper Missouri River—the Mandan, Hidatsa, and Arikara. These tribes were old-time gardeners who relied upon hunting for subsidiary subsistence. They lived in permanent villages constructed of large, semi-subterranean earth lodges. During the 18th century, and for the first decade or two of the 19th century, the Cheyenne settled down in earth lodge villages and grew corn, beans and squash in the manner of their new Indian neighbors. Their way of life was both sedate and sedentary.

Then, about 1760, the introduction of the horse opened new vistas for the Cheyenne. The plains were teeming with bison, an extremely rich source of food and derivative by-products. If they could only easily cross the great dry stretches between the widely scattered waterways with reasonable prospects of locating the herds, and be able to transport enough meat to the base camp, then the tribe could be sustained through the winter. Where men on foot found such prospects dim, men on horseback found them bright. By 1830, the Cheyenne were sufficiently equipped with horses to have completely abandoned the ancient village life of gardeners for the new nomadic life of hunters. Simultaneously, they were adding guns to their hunting and fighting equipage.

From 1857 to 1879 the Cheyenne were embroiled in almost continuous fighting with the Americans. The wars were not of their own choosing, but were often forced upon them by whites who were little disposed to discriminate among Indians. The Cheyennes were made to suffer for the more aggressive hostility of the Sioux, Kiowas and Comanches. They, too, were ultimately involved in the bitter struggles from which there was no escape but humiliating surrender and the lassitude of reservation life. A number of the fights were pitched battles between campaigning troops and sizable bodies of Indian warriors; some, such as those at Ash Hollow (1855) and Sand Creek (1864) were unprovoked assaults on friendly Cheyenne camps in which women and children were slaughtered along with the men who tried to defend them.

The Cheyennes played a large part in the repulse of Custer's attack on the Cheyenne-Sioux encampment on the Little Big Horn (1876) when Lt. Col. George A. Custer and five troops of the Seventh United States Cavalry were annihilated. In spite of this success, however, and the defeats inflicted on General Crook and his predecessors, the Cheyenne succumbed after the final destruction of the camps of Dull Knife and Two Moons, in 1877 and 1878. In the summer of 1878, under the leadership of Dull Knife and Little Wolf, three hundred Northern Cheyennes defied the United States Army by starting the long march home, to Montana. On January 9, 1879, after reaching their homeland and laying down their arms, many were killed, some recaptured. The survivors were placed on reservations established in Montana and southwestern Oklahoma.

Three Braves

This photograph is believed to have been taken by Will Soule in March 1869, at Camp Supply, Indian Territory. Here the 7th Cavalry stopped briefly with their Southern Cheyenne captives, en route to Fort Hays, Kansas, from Fort Sill, at the end of General Sheridan's winter campaign. The Indian at the right is Dull Knife (not the Dull Knife of the Northern Cheyennes, who last fought in 1879). The other two are Big Head and Fat Bear. Dull Knife and Big Head were killed at Fort Hays, 1869.

Three Braves

Ma-min-nic (Ma-nim-ick). Cheyenne Chief

Whirlwind

Brave

Squaw

Cheyenne camp, 1867

ARAPAHO

The Arapaho, like their neighbors the Cheyenne, were a typical Plains Indian tribe. They were not always so, however, since Arapaho traditions relate that they were once a sedentary, agricultural people. There is evidence that they once lived far to the northeast of their present area, somewhere near the Red River valley of northern Minnesota. In the 18th century they began drifting southwest, apparently in company with the Cheyenne who originally lived to the southeast of them. Here they came in contact with the village Indians of the Missouri, the Mandan and Hidatsa. From them the Arapaho are believed to have obtained many characteristic features of their ceremonial and social organization. About 1800 a division into northern and southern bands began to appear, although in 1806 it was reported that the Arapaho were still camped east of the Black Hills in South Dakota.

In the next few years the Northern Arapaho were camped on the edge of the mountains about the head of the North Platte, while the Southern Arapaho continued down toward the Arkansas. After 1840 they were generally at peace with the Cheyenne, Sioux, Kiowa and Comanche while they considered the Shoshoni, Ute and Pawnee their traditional enemies.

But during this period, as the myth of the Great American Desert fell beneath the feet of thousands of pioneers, the traffic on the Oregon and Santa Fe trails was increasingly harassed by the Plains Indians. To clear the paths of expansion, all tribes were to be moved either to the north or south of the Oregon Trail and assembled in two large colonies. The United States Bureau of Indian Affairs set out to conclude a series of treaties aiming to open safe corridors across the continent.

The first such compact was signed near Fort Laramie, midpoint of the Oregon Trail, on September 17, 1851. Among those signing were the Arapaho, Sioux, Northern Cheyenne and Crow who agreed to withdraw to clearly defined areas in Dakota, Montana and eastern Colorado and to cease making war on one another.

While the Southern Arapaho and their allies the Southern Cheyenne continued sporadic raiding during the 1850's, many of their chiefs believed it futile to resist the inevitable. By the Treaty at Fort Wise, 1861, they agreed to move to the area south of the Arkansas River in eastern Colorado. Even so some warriors refused to accept terms they considered dishonorable and it was not until 1864 that they had begun to tire of the incessant warfare. It was in this year, however, that the tragic incident occurred which helped send hundreds of vengeful Cheyenne and Arapaho warriors to attack many white settlements in Colorado. On November 29, 1864, as Cheyenne Chief Black Kettle and over seven hundred Cheyenne and Arapaho were about to surrender, they were wantonly cut down by a regiment of Colorado volunteers commanded by Colonel J. M. Chivington. While reports and conclusions vary, many women and children were slaughtered as they emerged from their lodges.

In the following year, 1865, campaigns by Colonel Henry Hastings Sibley and Brigadier General Alfred Sully succeeded largely in annoying but not intimidating the Indians, although one large Arapaho village, on the headwaters of the Tongue River (Wyoming), was dealt a costly blow by a sizable force under Major General Patrick E. Connor. For several more years Arapaho terrorized Union Pacific railroad construction crews and traffic on the

Smoky Hill Trail to Denver. But the destructive and costly Indian wars, combined with the growing sentiment for reform, led to the formation of a special peace commission in 1867. In October of that year the commission met with tribes of the Southern Plains and concluded the Medicine Lodge Treaty. The Indians agreed to cease fighting and withdraw to lands set aside for them in western Indian Territory. Part of this land had been seized from Indians of the Five Civilized Tribes who had sided with the Confederacy in the Civil War and had thus, reasoned Federal officials, forfeited their title.

These treaties failed to solve the Indian question or to bring peace to the Plains. While the Arapaho soon returned to the warpath with their allies, it was mostly the Cheyenne, Kiowa, Pawnee and Sioux who continued to fight hard for their land. The offensive that developed into the Red River War of 1874-75, under the command of General Philip H. Sheridan, led finally to a permanent peace on the Southern Plains; and the Arapaho, Kiowa, Comanche and Cheyenne retired for the last time to their reservations in Indian Territory.

Camp near Fort Dodge

This is an Arapaho (possibly Cheyenne) camp near Fort Dodge or Camp Supply, about 1869. The man with the sheet over his head is Horace P. Jones, Fort Sill Interpreter.

Yellow Bear

Known as "the most intelligent and soldierly Indian chief under Little Raven," Yellow Bear died of natural gas asphyxiation in the Pickwick Hotel, Fort Worth, Texas, about 1892.

Powder Face in War Dress

Little Raven. Head chief of the Arapahos

Big Cow

Yellow Bear *

Arapaho chief with squaw and child

Two sons of Little Raven. Little Bear and Shield (?). Probably at Camp Supply

Four Braves. Probably at Camp Supply

Three Arapahos

Powder Face with squaw and child

Little Big Mouth and tepee, near Fort Sill. Possibly a Cheyenne camp

Camp near Fort Dodge *

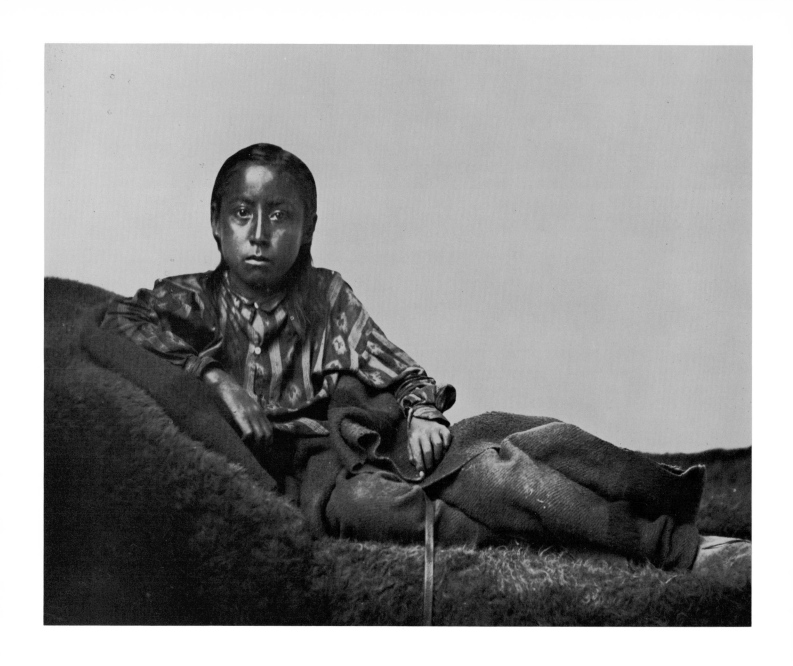

Son of Little Raven

Ba-e-tha and sister (also known as Zah-e-cha and Har-ke-i)

Shib-o-nester

COMANCHE

"The Comanche are not weak and blind, like the pups of a dog when seven sleeps old. They are strong and far-sighted, like grown horses. . . . You said that you wanted to put us upon a reservation, to build us houses and make us medicine lodges. I do not want them. I was born upon the prairie, where the wind blew free and there was nothing to break the light of the sun. I was born where there were no enclosures and everything drew a free breath. I want to die there and not within walls." So spoke Ten Bears for the Comanche at the Council of Medicine Lodge Creek in 1867. His oratory was forceful and eloquent. He represented himself as a man of peace, but he made it understood that he wanted no encroachment of either red men or white men upon the vast expanse of territory south of the Arkansas River which they considered their own.

However the reign of the Comanche on the Southwestern frontier was nearly over. For 150 years, since they had first come down from the north, at first alone and later with the aid of their Kiowa allies, the Comanche had been the lords of the Southern Plains. They had fought the Texans, made off with their cattle, burned their homes and effectively made their own lands unsafe for the white intruder. They had fought and beaten the Ute, Pawnee, Osage, Apache and Navajo. Thomas J. Farnham had written: "[T]heir incomparable horsemanship, their terrible charge, the unequalled rapidity with which they load and discharge their fire-arms, and their insatiable hatred make the enmity of these Indians more dreadful than that of any tribe of aborigines."

To themselves the Comanche were "the People." To the Ute the Comanche (Komantcia) meant "enemy"—or "anyone who wants to fight me all the time." In the sign language of the plains, the Comanche were known as the Snakes. When the Comanche were first definitely identified by the whites, they were so closely associated with the Shoshoni culturally and linguistically that it was impossible to distinguish between the two. At that time the Shoshoni covered a vast area, including most of Wyoming, Idaho, part of Utah and Nevada, Montana and part of western Kansas. By 1700 the Comanche and Shoshoni separated, the former drifting southward from the Rocky Mountain country while the latter gradually shifted to the north and west. With the horse, the Comanche achieved incomparably greater mobility; he mastered the buffalo; he had an exchangeable asset that made him a greater trader; he was transformed from an impotent infantryman into a fierce cavalryman. As a beast of burden and as a means of personal transportation the horse had a fundamental value to the Comanche. It enabled the hunter to provide plenty of food, clothing and shelter for his dependents, the raider to take more plunder, and the warrior to take more enemy scalps with less danger to himself. His life became exuberant, his culture efflorescent.

By 1800 the Comanche had moved into the territory of present eastern Colorado, southern Kansas, western Oklahoma and northwestern Texas. For control of this territory the Comanche waged a long but successful war with the Jumano allies of the French, the Spaniards and their Indian allies in New Mexico and the Apache to the south. The Comanche were among the first tribes of the plains to acquire the horse and the desire for a more abundant supply of these animals was certainly an important motive for moving closer to the source of supply—the Southwest. Meanwhile they had escaped the fate of the Shoshoni (who had been driven into the mountains) by drifting southward into relatively unoccupied area. Here they could consolidate their position and finally launch forth on a buffalo-based economy.

By the mid-nineteenth century Comancheria, the land of the Comanche, was the vast South Plains area bounded on the north by the Arkansas River, on the west by a line extending from the headwaters of the Arkansas River southward near the Mexican settlements of Taos and Santa Fe, on the southwest by the Pecos River, on the southeast by the white settlements in the vicinity of San Antonio and Austin—nearly 250,000 square miles. Although population estimates vary, well-informed contemporary observers believed that there were about 15,000 Comanche in 1850.

The American bison, or "buffalo" as it is commonly called, is not really a buffalo at all. It is one of the largest members of the family *Bovidae* that also includes cattle, sheep, goats and antelope. The first buffalo seen by Europeans was in 1521, and Pedro de Castañeda, the chronicler of the Coronado expedition, recorded that there were so many of them he did not know what to compare them to, except to the fish in the sea. The number of buffalo on the plains, before commercial slaughter began, reached a figure that staggers the imagination. On one occasion when the Great Herd moved north, it extended more than one hundred miles in width and was of unknown length. It was estimated conservatively that this herd contained over one hundred million head. By 1872 it became generally known that buffalo hides were marketable, the price being about $3.75 per hide. The railroad lines leading into the plains soon swarmed with hunters from the East. By wagon, horseback and afoot the hunters poured in and the slaughter was on.

Destruction of the herds went on at an increasing rate throughout 1876 and 1877. The greatest slaughter came in the winter 1877-78. More than one hundred thousand hides were taken in the months of December and January on the Texas range. The buffalo slaughter became an important issue with the public. Opponents fought it for sentimental reasons, or cited the great waste and the renewal of the Indian wars in support of their position. On the other hand, the buffalo

hunters, supported by a strong public opinion, insisted that they were rendering a great service in removing the buffalo from the Great Plains. Their position was summed up by General Philip H. Sheridan, in command of the Southwestern Department, before a joint meeting of the Texas Senate and House of Representatives in 1875: "Those men have done more in the last two years and will do more in the next year to settle the vexed Indian question than the entire regular army had done in the last 30 years. They are destroying the Indians' commissary; and it is a well known fact that an army losing its base of supplies is placed at a great disadvantage. Send them powder and lead, if you will, and for the sake of lasting peace, let them kill, skin, and sell until they have exterminated the buffalo. Then your prairies will be covered with speckled cattle and the festive cowboy, who follows the hunter as a second forerunner of civilization."

The reservation assigned to the Comanche and their allies by the treaty of Medicine Lodge in 1867 was nearly two million acres. There is no evidence that the Indians were ever convinced that it was best for them to deed away the greater of their lands, but the treaty signers probably realized that if they refused they would receive no annuity goods and would have to fight soldiers besides. Even so, only ten Comanche chiefs signed the treaty, representing probably no more than sixty percent of the Comanche population.

The first annuity day, December 30, 1868, saw great numbers of Comanche coming in to Fort Cobb on the northern edge of the reservation. But by that time the Cheyenne war had broken out along the Arkansas and the military feared that the Comanche and their allies might join the Cheyenne. To prevent such a possibility, they escorted those who had gathered southward to the vicinity of Medicine Bluff. There they established Fort Sill, driving the first stake of the new post on January 8, 1869. One small adobe building had been provided for the agency when Agent Lawrie Tatum arrived on July 1. This became the Agency headquarters for the Comanche, Kiowa and Kiowa-Apache.

Tatum, an unimaginative but courageous Quaker, believed that kindness and honesty would solve the Indian problem; he proposed to make the Indians secure in their legal rights, to locate them on the reservation and to assist them in agriculture and the "arts of civilized life." Experience proved however that as long as game was plentiful and the Indians could secure arms and ammunition from the traders, they could not possibly be kept on the reservation without the use of force. The government's "peace" policy was openly abandoned in 1872 as young warriors sought revenge for relatives killed by whites, for the slaughter of the buffalo—and they were very much determined not to live on the reservation.

Two years of bitter warfare followed, and by 1874, the Comanche (and the Kiowa and Cheyenne) saw that the old way was nearly over. As they sought comfort in the Sun Dance, a nativistic revival movement, Washington gave its consent for the army to attack the Indians in their own country, and from all sides troops poured into the Comanche and Kiowa range. Their concerted purpose was to drive all the Indians on the reservation or to kill them. While relatively few Indians were killed in these engagements (and virtually none of the braves were captured), their mounts and supplies were so depleted that they could not continue their existence on the plains; as cold weather approached, the bands straggled in one by one to surrender unconditionally.

The Comanche were finally beaten; they were placed in a concentration camp and once a day a wagon pulled up by the walls and hunks of raw meat were pitched over the fence, "like we were lions." The Indians had lost more than 7,500 head of horses and mules as a result of the campaigns. On August 5, Fort Sill had 1,076 Kiowa and 1,597 Comanche in confinement. The cultural change demanded of the Comanche was too rapid and too great for simple adjustment. Men trained for war and raiding and communal hunts found themselves idle, faced with the problem of adopting the white man's way of life. For some of them there was no problem. They simply refused to consider a change.

Additional information on those photographs marked with an asterisk may be found on page 112.

Bird Chief (Milky Way, Esa-habet, Asa-havey)*

Otter Belt

Esa-tou-yett (Asa-Toyeh, Grey Leggings)*

Ho-wear. A Yapparika Comanche chief, frequently at Fort Sill in the 1870's

Tosh-a-wah (Toshaway, Tosawi, Silver Brooch). First chief of the Penateka
Comanches and known for his peaceful attitude

Horse Back (Tuh-huh-yet, Nau-qua-hip, Champion Rider)*

Mow-way (Shaking Hand)*

Son of Horse Back (Too-hot-ko). An older son of Horse Back who was killed
in Texas by the Rangers

Comanche Camp, February 1875. This is believed to be Para-coom's (Bull
Bear) camp. Johnny Horseback may be the second Indian from the right

Two Squaws. Woman seated on buffalo robe is Looking-For-Something-Good (Cha-wa-ke)

Squaw

Three squaws and Papoose. *Left to right*: Wap-pah, Marn-me (Morn-me),
Qna-moth-kee. These women were taken prisoner by United States troops on
the Staked Plains, near Adobe Walls, Texas, 1868.

Bird Chief (Milky Way, Esa-habet, Asa-havey)

Esa-habet was known as a "friend of everybody" and often served as a contact between whites and Indians regarding the return of captives.

Horse Back (Tuh-huh-yet, Nau-qua-hip, Champion Rider)

Horse Back was born in Texas, about 1810, and was the principal civil chief of the Noconee Comanches. A signer of the Medicine Lodge Treaty and generally friendly to the whites, Horse Back was at the Fort Sill conference (1873) called to discuss the release of Satanta and Big Tree. Among those who spoke was Horse Back: "It makes my heart feel sad to see my two old friends prisoners here today.... I do not know what the other Indians here may think, but I am willing to comply with all I have heard. To make a white man of me, build me a house and give me a patch of land. But above all, release Set-tainte and Big Tree.... If my talk now falls to the ground I will leave here today with a crying heart."

Horse Back was one of the ten leading chiefs for whom houses were built at Fort Sill in 1876. In spite of the pride the Indians felt in their new dwellings, they would not live in them. Horse Back said: "Heap snakes in house."

Esa-tou-yett (Asa-Toyeh, Grey Leggings)

Esa-tou-yett had guided Colonel Grierson to the site of Fort Sill in 1868. At the 1873 Fort Sill conference Esa-tou-yett spoke: "... My heart cries to see my friends prisoners. I do not like to see this soldier post on my land.... I saw much prettier houses in Washington and could go into all of them.... This is a good day and when the sun goes down I would like to see the prisoners given to their people." Esa-tou-yett died and was buried at Fort Sill in 1878.

Mow-way (Shaking Hand)

A Kochateka chief, Mow-way surrendered at Fort Bascom, 1869. With several other Comanches he had been sent to Fort Leavenworth, from which, after a brief confinement, he had been released and taken to Fort Sill. He described the journey: "I supposed when we started that the soldiers were going to take us way off and then kill us.... But we ... were treated kindly.... When one of the Indians was taken sick ... they doctored him ... but he died, and then they did not throw him out in the grass for the wolves to eat, as I expected they would ... but (dug) a grave for him.... I could not understand why such mean people should be so kind to an Indian in sickness and after death...." Mow-way died near Fort Sill and is buried in the Post Cemetery.

Scalped Hunter near Fort Dodge

Harper's Weekly, of January 16, 1869, printed a woodcut of this photograph with the following caption: "On December 7 (1868) Mr. Ralph Morrison, a hunter, was murdered and scalped by the Cheyenne within a mile of Fort Dodge. Wm. S. Soule, an amateur photographer chief clerk in Tappin's Trading Company, took the picture. The officer is Lieutenant (Philip) Reade, 3rd Infantry. John O. Austin, Chief of scouts, is on the right. The photo was taken within an hour after the killing."

Osage Indian Scouts employed by the United States Army, under the command of Brevet Brigadier General Alfred Sully. In 1868 General Sully led several troops of the Seventh Cavalry across the Arkansas River in pursuit of the Cheyenne and Arapaho. It was this War of 1868 which led to the establishment of Fort Sill and, incidentally, to the assignment of Lieutenant Colonel George A. Custer to command the Seventh Cavalry.

Scalped Hunter near Fort Dodge

Indian camp, 1869

Cheyenne Camp

Osage Indian Scouts employed by the U.S. Army

Lone Wolf's Camp

Indian encampment, 1868

Pacer's Camp

INDEX OF INDIVIDUALS

PHOTOGRAPHIC CREDITS

Pages 54, 55, and 116 courtesy of The
Henry E. Huntington Library. Pages 16,
18, 19, 65, 80, 87, 119, and 120 courtesy
of Fort Sill Artillery Museum. All other
photographs courtesy of The History
Division, Los Angeles County Museum
of Natural History.